L. M. Montgomery

I Gave You Life

a novel
by
John Passfield

© 2024 by John Passfield. All rights reserved.
No part of this book may be reproduced, stored in a retrieval system, or transmitted by any means without the written permission of the publisher.

Anne of Green Gables is a registered trademark and a Canadian official mark of the Anne of Green Gables Licensing Authority, Charlottetown, PE. L.M. Montgomery is a registered trademark of Heirs of L.M. Montgomery Inc., Toronto, ON. Placement of this notice does not impute endorsement of this work by the Anne of Green Gables Licensing Authority or Heirs of L.M. Montgomery, Inc.

Cover image: A photograph of author L.M. Montgomery.
Cover design: Craig Passfield

Author's Website: www.johnpassfield.ca

For information, including permissions and bulk/retail purchases, please contact the publisher at customer.service@rocksmillspress.com.

Chapter 1

This will be the final Anne-novel. Not the last Anne-novel – that has already been written. No – this will be the final novel about Anne of Green Gables that I shall write. This one will come about the middle – not at the end. Anne will be somewhere in the middle of her life.

A person living in past and present simultaneously.

I have an idea for a story. A story about an orphan. I see red hair. She is riding on a buggy. A buggy with a sorrel mare. She is riding beside a man. An elderly man who strikes me as kind but quite perplexed. The girl is not what he had expected her to be.

To be

A young girl and an older person on a buggy.
A person who feels trapped inside a dream.
A character on the brink of her future life.

lost in

So are you actually going to write another Anne-novel?
After pledging so many times that you never would?
What has made you change your mind, if I may ask?

the picture.

The birches in the hollow turning golden.
A child revelling in the world of colour.
Strawberry apples growing in an old orchard.

Why did I not write the Anne-novels in order? Well – I had no desire to write any of them at all. Each one was, you might say, a product of necessity. Yes – 'necessity' is the word that I would employ.

A person for whom the past is never past.

An elderly couple. An orphan asylum. An application for a boy – a boy to do the chores around the farm. By mistake, a girl is sent. She is the girl who rides in the buggy. He will be Matthew – the man in the buggy. The girl will be the reason for the frown.

She was just twenty-one years old. She was lying in a bed. Her new young daughter was by her side. Her devoted husband was on the porch as the moonlight shone. Her husband and her daughter would be her whole life.

"Has Mrs. Montgomery only written just the one book?"
"All I've ever heard about is the one about Anne."

For some, it's just a dusty red road –
how you get from one place to the next.

A rabid quilting bee - some rays of darkness - wasn't too far off - this horrible empty feeling - bursting out of my bosom - the early scars still show - gather flowers to arrange - an anne without a me - bound for the rocks - all i saw was dark.

Good news Anne! Good news for you and for me! We are kindred spirits – you and I!

She never thought
of herself as
an orphan.

I never wanted to keep giving her life. I did not want to extend her life. I fought so hard to keep her young. Who did I fight against, you ask? Well, the most formidable fight of my life – was with Anne.
One for whom characters are people and people are characters.
Her name is Anne. Anne with an 'e'. She is talking as Matthew drives. She is opening up a world. Every word that comes from her lips I can hear in her voice. Anne is as alive to me as I am to myself. I am her and she is me. We are as close as any two souls could possibly be. We are writing her life together – Anne and I.

There was a young man who became a father. He had married the perfect girl. They were both as young as can be – and so in love. They lived in a little cottage surrounded by woods and flowers and fields. A red rose bush bloomed on either side of the door.

Starting a new Anne-novel.
Calling it *Anne of Ingleside*.

For some, it's merely apple-blossoms –
they always bloom at this time of year.

Look through her eyes - nothing but shadows - complete control - a life with no connection - between the covers - never saw the ring - something about a funeral - distilled from a drop of blood - she would imagine - print the edges in black.

Miss Montgomery! Miss Montgomery! I have been hoping to hear from you!

Wherever Az
would go
the sun
would shine.

Yes, I already have a title. Yes, it will certainly bear the name 'Anne'. *Anne of Ingleside* has a ring that will fall quite nicely, I believe, on thousands of ears.
One whose birth takes place inside a book.
Why not write her as a novel? Anne is as real to me as me. She is alive here on the island. All the places and people I know. Every situation and every incident. She has an attitude to life that has always been stifled in me. She is bursting out of my bosom. Anne is all the still-born Mauds I see in me. She is too good to waste in a story for a magazine.

A person under the sword of Damocles.
An author who wants to keep her character young.
A person who is falling apart at the seams.

Praying
at the meeting.
A cold wind
at the door.

So you say this will be the final novel in the series?
Are you willing to explain why this should be so?
How can such a kindred friendship ever end?

The seventy-fifth anniversary of the Leaskdale church. An invitation for Ewan to go back and give a sermon. Pleasant drive – cheerful meals – a backward glance at the good old times. Why do I have such a dreadful feeling that things will go wrong? Ewan sending along a note that we will go.

*Dark the night
and dark the wood.
Was when I travelled there.*

There was a little girl who was born on an island.

Their neighbours' business - are you in earnest - puts strychnine in the well - the ordinary observer - left the asylum - divinely beautiful - a lamp of guidance and promise - mistake came to be made - loved the world - resigned to my fate.

*An old churchyard by moonlight.
A little grey sparrow on a windowsill.
Gold and purple pansies to look at.*

Write a little story - you children will all be sep'rated - I never spent a cent - your ma is always raving - a ship, silent, white-sailed - a kidnapper of children - a strange shadow crept over the world - something you don't know - what your gift is worth - how strange the world was.

I have been jotting down notes for the adventures of Anne's brood. I shall make more notes for these episodes as I go along.
One who shapes her life as if writing a book.
Blocking out the chapters. Incident – characters – ending. Challenge – action – response. Situation 1, situation 2, situation 3. Writing furiously in my notebook. Sitting and brooding and writing again. I can put Anne in any incident – any challenge or any concern. I know exactly what she will say and what she will do. Lover's Lane – Shining Waters – every blossom on every tree. Anne is me coming alive as another me.

There was a man who met a little girl at a train station. He was looking for a little boy. He and his sister needed help on the farm. He looked around the station but he saw no little boy. Now how could such a simple plan go wrong?

"That book has been translated into all kinds of languages all across the world."
"People are reading it in Urdu and Senegalese."

For some, it's a magical canopy –
one little girl has called it The White Way of Delight.

A honey-comb of words - not prepared to live together - a lightbulb and a hunch - just another person - far too many questions - as clear as clear - gradually drifting out to sea - hoping to hear from you - feel a sense of importance

- to guard the door.

I signed a contract today with a publisher! I can give you further life! For a whole series of novels that will be about you!

*She was thrust into the world
inside out.
As far as she knew
she had been that way since birth.*

A kindred spirit? – a kindred spirit? Yes, Anne has been my very own kindred spirit, certain enough. More than any human being could possibly be. She has been with me for thirty-three years. She was there when my whole life changed. She was the *cause* of my great life-change. Becoming an author – becoming a wife – becoming another kind of Maud.
One who spends her entire life inside a book.
One last read from first to last before I send my Anne away. One more visit before I send her out into the world. Closing my eyes after I read the final page. As soul-mated as author and character could possibly be. A publisher – a publisher. Looking over my shelf of books. L. C. Page, 200 Summer Street, Boston, USA. What will he think when he reads these words? I wrap the package and tie the string and lick the stamps. I put my Anne on the counter, hidden carefully amid the outgoing mail.

There was a lady who lived on a farm. She was an elderly lady and fairly set in her ways. This elderly lady didn't care for girls. Well, girls were all right in their place. But a girl's place was not on this lady's farm.

Planning *Anne of Ingleside*.
What to have my Anne say and do?

For some –
it's a buggy-ride back to a long-lost home.

Was lost and not found - fell down, got up - released from our chains - the story of my life - searching the cupboard - about the only comparison - anything short of enchanted - at the back of the classroom - a magical canopy - strife and problems enough.

Oh that's wonderful, Miss Montgomery! A whole series of novels about me? I am so grateful to you that you have given me life!

*There was a certain water nymph.
Was born into the sea.*

Certainly Anne is my kindred spirit. But there is more to the riddle than that. At times Anne has been more me than me; at times I have walked alone, where she has not gone. Anne is more than a kindred spirit; Anne is less than a kindred spirit. Anne is me and Anne is not-me. We have been life-long friends and foes – Anne and me.

A pile of words on a desk awaiting form.

Sorting out the mail. A letter from L. C. Page – the Boston publisher! Is there more of Anne in my pen? Of course I shall write about my Anne! She is me in my better moments! She is me at the height of my reach! She is the better self who keeps the true flame of my soul!

"They say she gets letters from readers all the way around the world."
"I've heard she gets letters from Denmark and Japan."

A young girl

Two friends who share each other's thoughts.
A perpetual child who dwells in Avonlea.
A girl who wonders what her future will be.

used to sit and dream

Does Anne know that you are writing her final novel?
What would Anne say if she knew of your plan?
Do you consult her when you imagine the events of her life?

at her window.

But I have decided – the end is the end. This is the final novel for Anne. I am putting Anne behind me – for better or worse. *Anne of Ingleside* will be the final word.

A book whose walls are developing cracks at the seams.

A contract for *Anne of Green Gables*! An invitation to write a whole series of Anne-novels! I can't believe that this has happened! I'm just a girl from the island! Now my Anne will have a full life! She will live between the covers of a series of books! I had feared that she would be confined on a shelf in a hat-box! I can hardly wait to tell the good news to Anne!

Chapter 2

The writing of *Anne of Ingleside* will be a deliberate act of will. It is time to earn some money to pay the bills. I call up Anne as the Queen's Exchequer whenever I need her. She reluctantly comes when I call. She is the girl who pays the bills. If my readers only knew – they think of writing as so much fun. I am a queen begging pence of her parliament. I would get more satisfaction from scrubbing the floors.
Writing a series of novels in Cavendish, Prince Edward Island.
On a train on my way to Boston. I've never been to Boston before. What if Mr. Page changes his mind? I've had so many firm rejections. Why would one more be a cause of pain? I've been a writer since I was knee-high. I've had rejections from what seems like hundreds of magazines. Yes, and I've had my share of poems published too. So I am ready for Mr. Page. My skin is as tough as an alligator. Rejection would hurt Anne's feelings much more than it could possibly hurt mine.

To learn

A young lady who is sixteen and a half.
A mother who dies in childbirth.
Bottles of wine scrubbed and waiting to be filled.

the secret

Will you shine your spotlight on every one of the Blythes?
What will your story be for Jem?
What will your story be for Walter?

of immortal youth.

A candle glowing on a window sill.
A world which God imagined for his own pleasure.
Ferns and starflowers and lilies of the valley.

Rilla, Rilla, Rilla – what story do I have for Rilla? *A shameful and humiliating thing. Like one crushed forever. Happy and very well contented. Had no father and no mother. Gold and silver cake. Only mummy never laughed. Next thing to an orphan. Even God had failed.* Yes – yes. Rilla and the cake. It will be Rilla carrying a cake through the town.

An author who only writes about what he knows.

We have a handsome new minister in Cavendish. All the ladies divide the days between Sunday and the week. He is very handsome indeed. Good teeth, I remark to myself. From Highland Scots, but seems to have risen above it, though you can hear the Gaelic lurking behind his speech. He seems to enjoy my ebullient effervescence. His presence almost makes me forget that I am twenty-nine.

She looked down at the child in the crib. Mother, father, child. A scene repeated through endless eons of time. The general store would start to prosper. No matter what, they would be together every day of their lives.

"I hear she writes childish books for children."
"Wonder whether she ever thinks of writing for adults."

I am a household fly! I am swimming in an ocean! An ocean of pitch-dark ink! The ocean of ink has walls of glass! I cannot fly for the weight of the ink on my body and wings! I cannot climb out, for the glass is too slippery to climb! I swim around and flap my wings! I try not to imbibe any ink! Suddenly I am plucked up by my wings!

The up-side down and inside-out - two separate childhoods - your final conclusion - the mirror want to say - more to the riddle - slither in the depths - work without a plan - slashed by bramble - seal up the path - as frolicking angels.

Oh Anne. So nice to talk to you – so nice to hear your voice. It takes me back – it takes me back – to Avonlea.

Some day I shall return for a visit. We will definitely get together – you and I. We will spend the whole day together – have a do-you-remember day.

Two kindred spirits. Getting together in Avonlea. Not a care in the world – you and I.

Conceived
without parents
and sent to earth.

So many distractions – so many distractions. Bills to pay – correspondence to write. Ewan needs this – Chester needs that – only Stuart is able to function without borrowing my crutch. Time is whirling away like water down the sink. I will never be able to plan this novel of mine.

A publisher for whom books are a commodity.

Mr. Page comes into my bedroom. Of course, it's a room in his very own house. He has shown me all around Boston – introduced me to everyone. Oh how wonderful to sip the ambrosia of the literary world. He puts the contract on the little table and offers me a pen. I should be impolite and ask to read it. What would he say if I were to ask for more time? I suppose he would smile and say that all we really need is a handshake. I dip the pen in the inkwell and I sign.

And the young man was always filled with infinite promise. He was a young man whose shining star was always bright. Many fingers in many pies. His young wife was so in love. They were the perfect couple to everyone they knew.

Writing *Anne of Ingleside.*
Working out a story for Rilla.

I am placed on a blotter! I sink on the whitened swath! The ink on my body drags me down! I cannot walk nor fly! I determine that I shall live! I move my legs and scrape the ink away as best I possibly can! I shake my wings and the drops of ink fall on the blotter! I clean myself for what seems like hours and hours! I am almost ready to fly when, suddenly, I am plucked up by my wings!

Utter terror at the world - look back over the span - a connection between we two - the smashed vase - thinks no other thoughts - pretend they're somebody else - don't know what's wrong - some refuse to leave - as if it's your own - sense of the bitterness.

So – my Anne – just how have things been? It seems like such a very long time. I often think of you and everyone at Avonlea.

My life just seems to be so busy. There is barely a moment when I can just sit and reflect. Barely a moment when I can remember what life was like in Avonlea.

Oh you might feel as if I have neglected you. Please be aware that such is definitely not the case. But my life has been frantic – simply frantic – since those days.

To Az
the sunshine
always felt
like rain.

Yes – yes, I have it now. Rilla is only five. Susan is baking a cake – a gold and silver cake. A cake to send to the ladies at the church. To raise money for all the poor little boys and girls in the orphanage. Mummy and daddy are away from home. All the other children are busy. Rilla must carry the cake through the town to the Presbyterian church.

A reviewer writing a poison-pen review.

The new minister comes frequently to the Post Office. I am the envy of all the young ladies in the parish, as I manage to always be here when he arrives. Of course he can only come once a day – I cannot order extra mail. I have to explain such things when I say them. Our senses of humour don't seem to quite match. So – a little bit stiff in demeanor, perhaps, but quite charming when he manages to smile. What would he say if I were to tell him that I've written a book?

A best-selling author of many books.
A grandfather with a sarcastic tongue.
A mechanic fixing a tire in the pouring rain.

A man weighed
far, far down.
A beaten soul.

What will your story be for Di?
What will your story be for Nan?
What will your story be for Rilla?

Ewan talks of backing out – let them get someone else instead. But Ewan, you'll so enjoy it. A pleasant drive – some cheerful meals – a backward glance at the good old times. I offer to type his sermons so he can read them word for word. I talk him into resigning himself to go.

I lost the thing
I never had.
Was only in my dreams.

She was an orphan – or at least an orphan of sorts.

Their own concerns - turn out all right - a mighty foolish thing - the extraordinary observer - just went to work - dazzlingly clever - hadn't any real idea - the depths of despair - a morning like this - a name you gave it yourself.

Sunshine and soft winds for a few days.
A snowstorm dropping a white blanket over the world.
Children with inner-lives of dream and fantasy.

God was not satisfied - dramatized and personified - remote, inaccessible, a stranger - they'll never know - i'll lock you up - she had poisoned someone - the graveyard was full of shadows - missed seeing the notice - no woman would ever write - the whole story was sobbed out.

Do I want to write this novel? I feel like an ox attached to a wheel – waiting and waiting for my master's whip to descend. *Anne of Green Gables* wrote itself – the words kept flowing from my pen. I would pause for a second and then smoothly write page after page. Why is this novel so resistant? Why does the ink in my pen keep turning to ice?
A character who is grateful to be alive.
It is the day of publication. I have my own advanced copy – here in my hands. *Anne of Green Gables – Anne of Green Gables – Anne of Green Gables.* Not a soul in Cavendish knows except Anne and I. I have never said a word. I have taken a dream of mine and made a book. A world of ink and paper and sunlight. Mr. Page was full of predictions. Your Anne is a wonderful character. Readers will fall in love with Anne. He said that my life wouldn't be the same. Well, Mr. Predict-the-next Page – I shall prove you wrong.

So he talked to the station-master. 'I came to fetch a little boy. Me and my sister asked for one. The said they'd send him out from the orphanage. Me and my sister need some help on the farm.'

"She's a pedlar of nostalgia of earlier times."
"It's a market with a lucrative clientele."

In the ink-well, almost drowning! Swimming round and round in the ink! My body and wings are heavily-laden! The glass walls are impossible to climb! Plucked out and dropped on the blotter! I start to clean myself again! But then up and into the ink and plucked out again! I am exhausted – my strength is depleted! Swimming for life and then cleaning again! This is testing me to my limits! What a fiend my tormentor must be! I am dying of extreme exhaustion, but I shall clean and clean and clean! I shall struggle against my tormentor as long as I can!

Mend the coulter - sitting in the ditch - so prone to worry - make their deals in heaven - split in half - adult suffering and pain - grasp the snake - one who shapes her life - never saw the ring - open out for me.

One day I will return for a visit. I will spend a whole day in Avonlea. We are two kindred spirits, Anne – I need you as much as you need me.
Let's see – where shall we visit? What are the places we used to know? Where can we walk and talk together – just we two?
Lover's Lane – the Haunted Woods – Idlewild – Violet Vale – Bridle Path

– Crystal Lake. We'll have a picnic in Hester Grey's garden. Just you and I.

"How did you get that way?"
someone asked.
"Are you a circus performer
or an acrobat?"

Rilla is standing on the bridge. Such a shame to carry a cake. Such a terrible thing to do. Why are there orphans? – so many orphans? Why does Rilla have to help them? Why does Rilla have to carry a cake through town? Tilly Drake – stole a cake. Standing on the bridge. Miss Emmy coming along. The man she was going to marry has up and died. Snatching the cake out of the basket. What to do? – what to do? – what to do?
A reader who watches a movie of a book.
We agree to a secret pact – the Reverend McDonald and I. Not our families – not his parishioners – none of our bosom friends shall know. We are to marry when things are settled. When he has gone to Scotland to study. When my dear grandmother has died. When he finds a parish to his liking. When all is as both of us want it to be. Make your plans and see them through – on that we both agree. Neither of us wants to have any loose ends in our future life.

One day the lady's brother brought home a little girl. It was a girl, all right, as sure as one's eyes could see. She was sitting right there on the buggy, as plain as day. But why would her brother bring home a little girl? The plan – they had both agreed – was for him to bring home a little boy.

Working away at my story for Rilla.
Every character has a moment in the light.

"Mrs. Montgomery as a writer? Well, all I can tell you is that she always wrote in her bedroom. That was where she did her living. All her writing and all her banking and everything else that was important, you see. The rest of the house was 'out there in the world'. Occasionally, the bedroom door would be open – to get a cross-breeze in the heat. And she'd be writing at her desk – or sometimes pecking at the typewriter keys. He would be lying on the bed – a handkerchief around his head – still as death. And she would never make a sound, as if she was absorbed, don't you see, as writers do. But she was aware that I was there – dusting the fixtures in the hall – and she would call me to the door and say, 'Don't forget to go buy ice-cream for the cake' or some such thing. But no, she never shared her writing-thoughts with me."

Two fine oaks - as two new coins - must have been days - another kind of me - my life has been frantic - a tale of a different kind - everyone here seems - have a full life - nothing but sunshine - pretend they're somebody else.

Oh, Anne – my Anne – my Anne. We used to be so close. We felt that we could read each other's thoughts.

I will come and spend a whole day. We will visit the special spots. We will call it our do-you-remember day.

Oh I have had other kindred spirits. I know that you have had some too. But no two people have been as close as you and I.

One night the moon affected her.
And so on land she came.

Oh please, ye gods of writers. Wherever you dwell in the sky. Please come and fill my inkwell. Bring the magic of yesteryear. Bring me whatever potion I drank that day when *Anne of Green Gables* swam into my sight. You know that novel I told you about? – the one I call *Anne of Ingleside*? I have been planning the wretched thing for over a year.

A book which keeps its secrets well concealed.

I expected neither fame nor fortune. My Anne has given me both. Me – a simple girl from the island. Newspaper articles – columns of reviews – letters from readers. Every busybody on the island trying to guess who might be who. Who is Marilla? – who is Matthew?, and, above all – who is Anne? Several people have claimed that they gave me the whole idea. Privacy gone – money gained. Royalty cheques of a size that I couldn't have imagined in my dreams.

"It's hard to relate to a world where people still use horses and buggies."
"She should write about the world that we're living in now."

Matthew, Anne and Marilla

A son who turns his mother out of his house.
A girl who marries the man of her utmost dreams.
A two-hour car-ride that takes all night.

in a photograph

What will your story be for Shirley?
What will your story be for Gilbert?
Will you find it hard to think of a story for Anne?

in front of
Green Gables.

Why such a dreadful secret? Why does Rilla feel so alone? Why does nobody notice? Why is there no one to talk to? Why is she tired of being herself?

Why a disgrace to those she loves? Why does Anne say that the story will not be told?

An author who goes through hell to write a novel.

I used to be so good at spelling. Now the letters just slip from my mind. Is it 'Ewan' or is it 'Ewen'? Which one better suits the man? Is it 'McDonald' or is it 'Macdonald'? It will be my name forever, so I'd best learn how to spell it or I won't know who I am. Well – plenty of time to get to know my husband. I shall find out more – much more – than just his name. It is no matter – it is no great matter. Very soon we two shall be married and all will be well.

Chapter 3

Bright and early in the morning. The time when I get my best ideas. A cup of tea – plenty of paper – my inkwell and my pens. I am an alchemist of many years standing. I shall transform this stack of blank paper into a book. There is a crowd outside my workshop. They are chanting the name of Anne. Clutching their pennies in their hands. A new Anne-novel will be a treat. *'Anne of Ingleside'* has a ring that pleases me.
Writing a series of novels in Leaskdale, Ontario.
'The Leaskdale manse' – 'the Leaskdale manse'. A charming phrase that I keep repeating. It is the first place that I can truly call my home. Mine and Ewan's of course – mine and Ewan's – he is the reason that I am here. The people here are very gracious. 'Treat the manse as if it's your own.' It will be mine in each nook and cranny. I have saved nicknacks for twenty long years. Ewan and I shall start our family. We shall be snug and warm inside. I'll set my two china dogs to guard the door.

To write

Letters sent from Denmark and Japan.
A minister who mumbles and sits down.
A doctor who prescribes endless pills.

some clever

Why do you keep writing novels about Anne Shirley?
Is it the money or the fame or something else?
Why do you say that each Anne-novel will be your last?

little things.

Sweet peas growing in the garden.
A delightful spiciness in the air.
Elfin chimes coming through the frosty air.

Two rows of little puppets on my shelf. The family of Anne and Gilbert. A dining-room table with laughter all around. Anne, Gilbert, Jem, Walter, Nan, Di, Shirley. And a new one – yes a new one comes to town. Bertha Marilla Blythe – Rolly Polly – Rilla for short. I will shine my cheerful spotlight on each one.

Writing the first page of the novel, Anne of Avonlea.

A letter from L. C. Page. He is pleased that *Anne of Green Gables* is doing so well. A good idea, he writes, to have a second Anne-novel ready while the first is enchanting the crowds. He praises Anne as a character. So delightful – so unique. He is sure that the reading public will clamour for more. Should I tell him that Anne enchants her author no more?

What will be my little daughter? What will she grow up to be? When I am well I will sing her lullabies. Gather flowers to arrange in the vase. When this cough that I have in my lungs goes away.

"Reverend Montgomery doesn't seem to have much to say."
"Maybe he only has something to say when he's in the pulpit."

Somebody poisoned our family dog. Why would anybody do such a thing? Somebody gave it something poison for it to eat. Dad says it might have been an accident. Mom says at least it didn't suffer. We found it dead on the porch. All we kids loved the dog. Why did somebody have to poison it? I don't want to live in a place where you have to bury your dog.

Some truths are being told - waiting in the wings - nothing left of the diamond - fall where they may - remote and unreal - darkness hid him - arrangement in the contract - decisions have already been made - out of its own entrails - bring me a daisy.

Oh Mrs. Montgomery – oh Mrs. Montgomery – so nice to hear from you. I can hear your voice as if you are in the room. Yes – yes – things are fine in Avonlea.

Oh I hoped you would come back. You hoped you would be able to. That is perhaps the last thing you said to me.

You said that if all went well. If all your plans worked out as you hoped. You crossed your fingers, you said, and then you made a wish.

An Achilles
without
an Achilles heal.

So what is this other row of puppets? Who are the others who make up the town? Neighbours, patients, fellow-students – living in the shadows of the

Blythes. What can I have them do and say? All of the Blythes will have happy endings. But what of these – these vague not-Blythes? Any room for some rays of darkness amid the light?

A publisher who asks an author for more of the same.

Flesh of my flesh – bone of my bone. Nursing at my breast. A living link to every person who has ever been born. A link with every person who shall ever be born, from now until the end of all time. Chester Cameron Macdonald. All hail the first-born son. You shall carry that name for the rest of your earthly years. What will you be? – what will you do? – you who sleep so soundly in your crib? You who have come into my life? Why have dreams of a black coffin accompanied you?

And one day his young wife gave birth to a little girl. He wanted to bring joy and comfort into her little life. His bosom swelled as he stood on the porch in the moonlight. His wife and new daughter were the finest things in his life. Tears rolled down his cheeks as he thought of them.

Starting a new novel about Anne.
Calling it *Anne of Avonlea*.

Anne is so visibly tired. Gilbert is obviously depressed. Anne tells me the aunt is poisoning their lives. The aunt never had a friend in her whole life. Her name should be Blight not Blythe. Squeezing the laughter out of every family meal. The aunt has money and a home of her own. I'm advising Anne to turn her out. Throw the mutineer overboard and save the crew.

Hear me shout and scream - let me think a while - no practical bearing at all - sigh and sympathize - never hold water again - a ridiculous, petty-fogging argument - whose armour is thin - dark the wood - slither in the depths - the shelves of my memory.

Well – nothing has happened since you left. I am surprised that you should ask. No – nothing new has happened in Avonlea.

Marilla's eyes are giving her trouble. Gilbert gave up his place at the school. I gave up the scholarship and stayed here – in Avonlea.

Each day I go to the end of the book. I stand on the very last page. I try to look out from Avonlea.

Wherever Za
would go
the rain
would fall.

I sit at my desk every morning. My title is *Anne of Ingleside*. I cannot work without a plan. A plan is a blueprint for an adventure. A plan is a path to follow as I write. I need a plan – I need a plan. I have nothing on this page. Is it Anne who is resisting? Am I contesting with my Anne? Does she want this novel written – or does she not? I shall sit here every morning – me and my paper and my pens. I always make a plan before I write.

A reviewer who seeks to control the literary crowd.

Working all summer on the new Anne-novel. I believe I shall call it *Anne of Avonlea*. I always work to a plan. Good things happen when I have a plan to draw me on. Characters, incidents, endings. Some things familiar – some things new. Episodes in a narrative string. By the fall, I should be ready to start writing the words.

A writer who sues her publisher.
A person holding the fragments of another together.
A Hollywood movie set in New England.

His dusty robe – his sandals worn.
His sunburned face – his windblown hair.

Why have you written the Anne-novels out of order?
Should she not have grown in stages, along with her fans?
Are the novels written for you or written for Anne?

No sleep for Ewan last night. No sleep for me as well. Trying to find a replacement for Ewan, but it's tomorrow and no one can go. I type the sermons and beg him to read them word for word. He gets angry and blusters and shouts that he is fine.

A ring was lost
so I heard tell.
Was lost among the woods.

She had two childhoods – two separate childhoods.

Going out of avonlea - don't know a single thing - a good home and schooling - no commonplace soul - imagine something worthwhile - angelically good - must be in a dream - try to imagine - I can hear the brook laughing - casting a spell over me.

Rain drops lying on nasturtium leaves.
Yellow-green ferns from the maple grove.
Small winds purring in the valley.

Colourful pageantry of life - everything in his small world - delicately balanced organic chemistry - had to resign herself to the inevitable - reasons best known to himself - had some dreadful secret - a spasm of uncontrollable panic - tried to make them believe - a white blanket over the world - something important to tell her.

Something about an obituary – and 'obichery' – an 'obitchery'. Now what could that possibly be? Something about a funeral. Whose funeral could it be? A quilting bee with chatter. What would the chatter be all about? A boy and his dog. Which boy – which dog? Shadows – nothing but shadows. Hiding and calling out in the dark. I scribble these fragments on my page. Oh why will these shadows not come clear for me?

A character who wonders what her new life will be.

Well, what else should they write on my mail, Ewan? 'To the lady of the manse, in care of Reverend Macdonald?' They would not know who that is. These are letters about my books, Ewan – these are letters to the author of 'Anne'. I am two people, Ewan – in Leaskdale I am 'Mrs. Macdonald' – better known as 'the Minister's wife'. In the rest of the world I am known as 'the author of Anne' – I am the author of the girl who pays our bills. Yes, I am two people, Ewan. Be grateful, Ewan, that you are only one.

The station master wasn't too helpful. Told him there wasn't any boy. The only orphan off the train was a little girl. There she was sitting on the shingles. Told him he'd better go over and talk to the little girl.

"Mrs. Montgomery does most of the talking."
"Her husband seems content to just nod and smile."

It's a bright red parasol. I am holding it in my hand as we walk along. A gift that her mother gave to Nan. Nan won't be the same tomorrow. This will shake her out of her shoes. If Nan is not Nan then her mother isn't Anne. Now I'll *have* to tell her the story. The story isn't really true. I never meant for things to go this far.

Are we good enemies - how many chapters - is not anne's island - all is sunny and fine - i cannot climb out - never a drop of blood - no idea where all of this would lead - do you consult her - go and live somewhere else - a hound for cash.

But you are the writer, Mrs. Montgomery. Nothing could happen without your consent. You created everything here.

You created every person in Avonlea. You created every event. Nothing will happen until you write another book.

Oh it must be wonderful to be a writer. To sit by a window and dream and dream what life could be. And dip your pen into the inkwell and turn it all into words.

The tough shell of her hide
was where her insides
should have been.
The soft and tender
defenseless core
was facing out.

But what about Anne? What about Anne? What is the story for my Anne? Anne as an adult – Anne as a mother – Anne as a wife. Anne from thirty-four years old to forty years. I don't find her in my mirror – that is not where I'll find my Anne. Do I want Anne as an actual person – sitting beside me, here in this room? Will I find her in the closet – where I left her on the shelf? – awaiting her cue to dance and sing as I pull the strings?

A reader who is transported outside the self.

Chapter Eight – Chapter Eight – Chapter Eight of *Anne of Avonlea*. Writing – writing – writing. Here at the window, where I always write so well. I shall call it the Golden Picnic. The woods – the pool – the dancing. The girls as dryads or as nymphs. This chapter will be the heart – the very heart – the Anne-heart – of *Anne of Avonlea*.

What was going on at the orphanage? Don't they know farm work is for boys? Only a city-person would ask for a girl. What was wrong with Mrs. Spencer? What was she thinking when she sent a little girl?

Finishing *Anne of Avonlea*.
Never again – no never again a novel about my Anne.

I am sitting on a pile of shingles. I have been here for quite a while. Mrs. Spencer dropped me off and told me to wait. I said goodbye to the asylum. I'll say goodbye to this ugly dress. I will live on this wonderful island and call it home. In the distance I see a buggy. It is a man with a sorrel mare. I was looking for a couple. An elderly man and his sister. But now I already know that this is the man. So I am sitting here and waiting. Sitting and waiting for Matthew to speak to me. I am sitting and waiting with all my might and main.

Must be a closed book - told him anyway - his stranglehold on mine - see myself at centre stage - out there in the world - my task is to spotlight - you didn't ask - to expel my twin - arguing in the dark - what are we to do.

But you say you have some plans. You say you have good news. It was something about a contract which you have signed.

So you can give me further life! Oh Mrs. Montgomery – I can barely believe! I was afraid I was going to spend my whole life at sixteen and a half!

So what will happen with Marilla's eyes? Will I go away to school? I can't imagine what the rest of my life is going to be!

But no one found she waiting.
No great love encountered she.

Oh why can I not make any progress on *Anne of Ingleside*? Why can I not make it go? I wind it up and set it down and – nothing happens. What is Anne as an adult? I have written about her before. I search the shelves of my memory. How did I ever write those books? How did I ever write of an Anne who is not a child?

A book which sits on a shelf for years and years.

Oh I love to go to Toronto. The exhilaration of a trolley ride. Ewan seldom comes along with me – he doesn't enjoy it at all. Not a bone of sophistication – nor a sliver of art in his soul. But if he were to win a city parish – we could move to the centre of town. It would make him feel more successful – he would learn to love city life. A whole new world would open out for me – something different every day. Listen to a speaker – attend a play -- take part in a lively conversation about something other than Ewan's church. Oh, how I'd love to wake up in Toronto some sunny day.

"They were very successful as a ministerial couple."
"Much admired in Leaskdale and in Norval for many years."

Every day

Two people who bring no baggage to a new town.
An old lady who doesn't care for girls.
A girl who lets a genie out of a bottle.

the girl looked out

Will *Anne of Ingleside* be the same kind of novel as all of the others?
Or will *Anne of Ingleside* somehow be different from the rest?
Which of these reasons makes you want it to be your last?

upon the world.

I am a school teacher – harassed and harried. Facing a forest of waving arms – all clamouring for attention. Ewan, Chester, L. C. Page, William Arthur Deacon, Morley Callaghan, Raymond Knister, Violet King. Each one shouting and waving their hands in my face. And there – at the back of the classroom – sits the new little girl. Bright eyes – freckles – red braids. She is waiting for her adventure. Hoping I'll notice her through this forest of waving arms.

Writing the last page of the novel, Anne of Avonlea.

Anne of Green Gables is finding its way. It is an avalanche of applause. Sweden, Holland, Poland – Anne is travelling around the world. I was reluctant to write about Anne. I told myself – never again. But Mr. Page is so persuasive. The royalty cheques are welcome indeed. The same financial arrangement for *Anne of Avonlea*.

Chapter 4

So what do we have here? – what – do – we – have – so far? Ann Shirley as a woman who is about half-way through her life. The middle years of adulthood, shall we say? Anne as a wife – married to Gilbert. Ann has children – by number, five. Six by the end of the book – an Anne with another little one on the way. My task is to spotlight each member of the Anne-family in turn.

An author jotting an idea in a notebook.

Working in the mornings. Making lists and lists and lists. Lists of characters – lists of predicaments – list of places where events can take place. Lists of titles that have an appeal. Feeling low and very uneasy. Finding it hard to get out of bed, but I force myself to get up and get back to work. It was easier by far, when I was waiting for Chester. We are all sent from heaven – some to scourge and some to bless. But we come with no indications of which is which. Perhaps a delightful little girl is on the way.

To still

A time-limit on bread and butter and milk.
An author who talks to her character.
A book in which every word is wrong.

believe

Do you imagine Anne to be an actual person?
Do you summon her up whenever you need to talk?
Doe she answer you every time you call?

in fairy land.

Bottles of milk kept cool in the brook.
A sleigh filled with straw and furry robes.
Two girls making necklaces of roseberries.

Little Jem. A story for Jem. What am I going to have my little Jem do?

Wrongs surged up. Overwhelmed him. Made up his mind. Scowled more blackly. The use of going on living. I have Jem. I have my Jem. Jem is a little boy who feels like running away.

An author who turns acquaintances into characters.

Sitting and writing every day. Feeling the need to write about characters other than Anne. None of them sell as well as Anne, but they are companionship for me. Once in a while, a note from my publisher. 'I assure you there is a ready market for Anne.' Every sign-post points to a very familiar path. L. C. Page and Anne are the horses who pull my cart.

Black hats and black coats. Black crepe on every arm. Black harness on the horses. Black plumes above their heads. Slowly wending one's way to the cemetery at dawn.

"The Anne-books always get such glowing reviews."
"Not from her fellow writers in the Toronto CAA."

How did I get into this dream? I am living in a town where a family's dog gets poisoned! I am living in a town where a mother slaps a child's face for every little thing! I am living in a town where a person can be buried alive! How do I get out of this dream?

Nothing in the world too good - set me free - one last chance - wrested from my hand - trapped between the covers - something very important - she can't help but see - willing to explain - to take my chances - but now i know.

Oh, Anne – much has happened since we were together. It seems, sometimes, as if I have lived my whole life. If I were to tell you, I would not know where to begin.

But my life must be a closed book. I must never tell you a thing. No gossip across the fence for you and me.

Better I tell you nothing at all. Better you never know what my life is like. Better you never come to know what my life has been.

No fear
of the hammer
or the knife.

I must sit and catch my breath. My heart is threatening me. There are dreams that we people dream that remain unknown to us. These dreams occur in the deepest darkest pit of the night. They colour the very fibre of our being. They put a twist on every thought we ever have. So, too, are some of our experiences. Some things happen that sear us so deeply that the mental wounds are always raw, so the thickest mental bandage is what we apply. We drive them deep-deep down to the darkest pit of our minds. To the level of the most frightening, most unknown dreams.

A publisher who takes a book from an author's hands.

Yes, there were eight hundred people, Ewan – yes there were seven newspaper reviews. Oh, but Ewan – please consider – they ask me to go and speak and so I do. They are eager for news of the island – they are eager to hear about Anne. My talks are not to be compared with your sermons – no, you are not to think in that way. Consider my writing to you as is Anne to me. As a nicknack in a cupboard – taken out and dusted off for a moment or two – admired as an interesting keepsake – everyone crowds around to look – then put away in the dark and forgotten again.

So, what is a father? What does a father do? He sits by the fire, reading his paper. He smokes his pipe of an evening. His little girl sits and plays on the rug at his feet.

Writing *Anne of Ingleside.*
Working out a story for Jem.

How did I get into this dream? I am living in a town where boys torture miserable scrawny cats! I am living in a town where a badly-burned baby is rushed to the hospital! I am living in a town where children tell other children vicious lies! How do I get out of this dream?

Made no sense at all - a child-like bubble - contains the whole of my life - no more than a tiny beacon - seems to have risen above it - make it seem very real - could not see my way - less than a kindred spirit - darkness hid him - people adrift on stormy seas.

Am I married? Who is my husband? Is he the man of my utmost dreams?
Do I have children? Girls or boys? Or some of each?
Left the island? Living abroad? Or just down the road from you, in P.E.I.?

To Za
the rain
always felt
like sun.

Little Jem does not feel loved. No one listens to little Jem. Perhaps the family is too big. Perhaps if Jem were the only child he would have his due. He wanders around the house. All are busy or not at home. Why does no one ever pay attention to Jem? Who would miss him if he ran away from home?

A reviewer who plays the literary stock-market.

Reading, reading, reading – reading an hour or two every day. Whenever

I can spare a moment or two from my chores. Reading the old books and the new. Re-reading books I have read before. Books of authors I meet in Toronto and books of people from far-away lands. Lands of enchantment – stories of intrigue – voyages ending on sunny shores. Yes, a book can disappoint – a book can bitterly disappoint – but I can sweep it from my life. I threw a horrible book away just the other day. Do authors flinch when their books are treated this way?

A neighbour who knows everyone's business.
A little girl delivering a cake.
A lady who feels like a squirrel inside a wheel.

I swear was blood
came out his eyes.
Was mixing
with his tears.

Is she the Anne of the husband and children?
Is she Anne as a little girl?
Is she the Anne of all of the novels or just of one?

In the car on the way to Leaskdale. Evan insisting he knows the roads. Driving miles and miles in circles as I tell him we're taking wrong turns. Insisting we're just around the corner – insisting that he is fine. He used to know these roads like the back of his hand.

The ring would glow
when all was dark.
Was glowing in the woods.

One was enchanting and one was mundane.

Going a considerable distance - surprised at nothing - felt her doubts and fears - stray woman-child - your imaginations come true - eyes that saw visions - haven't very far to go - a horrible sickening feeling - such a stray waif - have you ever noticed - another hope gone.

A big lawn with magnificent trees.
A boy opening a door in a brick wall.
A string of sleigh bells which make chimes.

Prized house made of shells - a great white charger - a fortuitous concatenation of atoms - an agony of indecision - said the bitterest things out loud - never lost her way - been a real sickly winter - the truth pops out - like a slap in the face - safely back at ingleside.

I sit at these meetings of the CAA. Forgive me, Lord, for my contempt. They call themselves Canadian – so am I. They call themselves authors – so am I. But I am something that they are not – I write books that people read throughout the world. And my readers reach out to me. I get letters from people in Denmark and Japan. People tell me how affected they feel. They all feel as if they are living their lives with Anne. I reach out beyond myself and my tiny circle. I give these people Anne – I give them life.

A character who is ready for any eventuality.

Oh, the failure of Ewan's mission. Why did Ewan not listen to me? Ill advised – ill advised – from the very start. He was so full of enthusiasm – he was as high as a hot-air balloon. But he doesn't know his parishioners very well. Farmers will not give up their money – not for China – not for Japan. Every penny is so hard-come-by. They would sacrifice for a neighbour – work their fingers to the bone – but they will never – ever – part with their hard-earned cash. Charity begins and ends at home. Ewan's balloon has drifted to earth in a farmer's field.

How do you talk to a little girl? How do you talk to any female? He had never talked to a female in his life. Well, his sister was a female. Guess he had to admit to that.

"The Moderns complain that she doesn't write about grit and grime."
"How can she write about grit and grime with the life she's had?"

How did I get into this dream? I am living in a town where a little boy can drown in a rain-water hogshead! I am living in a town where a person can die of a disease barely known to the world! I am living in a town where children grow up to be adults! How do I get out of this dream?

Black crepe on every arm - whether this is actually so - ignoring ghosts - glad to leave behind - why are there orphans - what they're escaping from - not what she seems - cheated her of her rights - something very important - slowly sinking down.

I am a writer – of course you know. I am the writer who created the character – Anne Shirley – *you*. I gave life to you and – in a sense – you gave life to me.

All I can tell you – at this time – is that I have signed a book-contract. The publisher is very pleased with your book – *our* book, Anne – the book we wrote together, you and I. The book will be printed and sold – and read – throughout the world.

Yes, I signed a contract today. And there was a clause that practically glowed. It was an authorization, Anne – a giving of permission, if you will – to write a whole series of novels – all about you.

The village children
would throw stones at her
and poke her with a stick.

Jem is gone. Jem is gone. He is nowhere in the house. Susan searches everywhere. Anne comes home and does the same. They are worried in the extreme. Word is spread throughout the town. The men are fixing to drag the pond. Has anyone seen Jem, the oldest boy up at the Blythe's?
A reader for whom a character is a personal friend.
Visiting ministers are always so successful. If they were not, of course, they would not be making the rounds. Younger-seeming – handsomer-looking – more buoyant than the resident cleric. They sparkle and dazzle while Ewan glowers and frowns. They flutter hearts and cause the collection plate to jingle. Ewan plods along in harness – making his usual rounds. Once in a while he heaves a sigh. Old Dobbin is getting tired of pulling the plough.

And this little girl had a lot of ridiculous ideas. What was all this about the most tragic thing that ever happened? What was all this about the White Way of Delight? What was all this about the Shining Lake of Waters? So many detrimental thoughts in one little head.

Working away at my story for Jem.
Jem of the lost and found again.

"Her oldest son was a holy terror. Yes – Chester – the oldest son. She put up with a lot from him. If you ask me, more than a parent should. As if ignoring it would make it go away. Well, we all know what becomes of a plan like that. He grew bolder as he got older. I overheard him challenge his dad. Where I come from a boy would always fear the belt. Petty thievery, I would call it. Things would be missing from the house. No, I was never accused – no, never once. She knew – I knew she knew. Like the time that was intolerable. I had to protect my little girl. I told her I didn't trust her son to know how to behave. Well – she didn't want to believe – but it was all there on her face. She just couldn't say out loud that she agreed. Well, this was the one I couldn't live with. I had to protect my little girl. I had always enjoyed working there – Mrs. Montgomery was good to me. I gave notice that I would leave. She said she was sorry to see me go, but her face was saying what else am I to do?"

We're taking wrong turns - the need for a change - jostle at the feed-bowl - petty cares of petty days - a girl wishing - mental wounds are always raw - aim your flashlights - not to be thought of - have no access to - darkness just might damage.

But of my own life – not a word. Much time has passed since you and I have talked. Much has happened to me about which you shall never know.

Of *your* life much will be known. I am about to start a new Anne-book. But over *my* life I must draw a veil of silence.

I must sound like Mata Hari – all the intrigue of a fictional spy – you must think I am acting like a character in a book. But I assure you that it is best that I keep some secrets from you, Anne. I am doing what is best for both of us – you and me.

But now her gills had lungs become.
A nymph no more was she.

Mrs. Raymond Knister. Her brown eyes warm and aglow. Her young husband at her side. In the flower-display section at the Canadian National Exhibition. We stop and exchange pleasantries. My husband often speaks of you. I'm sure he does – I'm sure he does. He also writes of me in magazines. About how Canada has never produced any characters who are able to stand with their literary counterparts on the world stage. And, at my elbow, I introduce the young couple to Anne.

A book which sits on a reader's lap and purrs.

People here are quite restrained. Standoffish, one might say. They lack the charm of the locals in P.E.I. Their eccentricities well-hidden from the minister's wife. I miss my old vantage-point in the post office. No one there had any other side to show. Or if they did, they didn't see any need to hide it from the girl who was too dreamy to notice anyway. Not a word of unrestrained chatter or an ounce of unfettered charm. I won't get any books out of Leaskdale at all.

"I don't care whether she writes realistic novels or not."
"I'd rather read L. M. Montgomery's sunshine than Morley Callaghan's rain."

Maude and Anne

Modern poems about dung and latrines.
A nicknack taken out and dusted off.
A young man who is studying the law.

in a photograph

Is she an Anne who is entirely independent?
Is she an Anne who only says what you want to hear?
Why do you speak to her and why does she speak to you?

with Matthew and Marilla.

Why does a child feel so unloved? How can a parent not seem to know? What does he need? What does he get? Why does life sometimes seem hollow? Every toy a child could want? Maple frosting at every meal? Why this horrible empty feeling? Why the need to be somewhere else? Why do so many people live with such fear?

A writer spinning a poem out of his entrails.

I make in the neighbourhood of three thousand dollars a year. You – Ewan – make eight hundred dollars – flat. You like the butter on your bread – you like the jam on the butter on your bread. I was a writer before I met you – I was earning my daily bread. You are admired – you are looked up to – the congregation respects your word. You have everything here that you ever said you would want. Don't lose any sleep over nothing. Think of Anne as an aunt who sends money – other than a 'thank you', nothing ever need be said. Has anyone spoken of this to you? – surely no one has ever implied that *I* pay all the bills? It doesn't bother *me,* Ewan, if it doesn't bother *you.*

Chapter 5

There will be two groups of characters. Two cycles, shall we say. The major note will be the Anne-cycle – the Ingleside-cycle – of Anne and Gilbert and their brood. The minor note will be the not-Anne cycle – the non-Ingleside cycle – the anti-Ingleside cycle, if I may. The two cycles will interact as the novel goes on.
A novelist making a series of possible plans.

Hugh Alexander Macdonald. We lay you in your grave. Not as a soldier – not as a sailor – not as a casualty of war. You are the boy who died at birth. You have orphaned your own mother. Child of my daydreams – child of my womb – child of all the hopes and dreams I had for you. You shall never bring me a daisy – you shall never show me a worm. I shall nevermore give you a hug – give you a kiss. You shall lie in the cold, cold grave until I come, some day, to join you. I felt I gave you my sense of humour – my sense of the bitterness and the strife. We never had a chance to laugh and cry.

To spend

A pack of lies which are spoken at a funeral.
A canopy of white blossoms on a road.
A person who has suffered crushing defeats.

a night in

Do you wish that *Anne of Green Gables* stood alone?
That there were no other novels that told the story of Anne?
That she had remained a little child for the rest of her life?

a masquerade.

Decorating a room with maple branches.
Twilight under a great high-sprung sky.
Scrumptious fun playing at dinner time.

So nice to be writing again. A year of planning – on and off. Jotting notes and fragments and phrases, but not so easy to write when the mind is not free and clear.

Writing the first page of the novel, Anne of the Island.

Another Anne-novel? L. C. Page is a hound for cash. He is baying at me to make a new novel of Anne. Do I want to go back to Avonlea? I find it harder, each time, to have to come back here, to the every-day. Anne is not my favourite character. I have tried – oh how I have tried – to get away, as much as possible, from Anne. Anne and L. C. Page are the two who dog my heels. However, Anne is the one who pays the bills.

I've heard it said that if one's mother dies before you know her, that you end up hardly missing her at all. But this is not true. Life is never – ever – the same. There's a hollow spot inside. You miss her every minute of every day.

"Her oldest son is a cad and a petty thief."
"The maid says he takes anything that isn't nailed down."

Not exactly Cain and Abel. Alexander and his brother, Jeffery. One made money and one made friends. The rich well know the value of a dollar. Wouldn't lend his brother a hundred dollars for an operation. Gave him a hundred dollars for a tombstone after he died. What is the lesson? – what is the lesson? Let me think for just a while. There is no daisy in the field but has a flaw.

Just red for no reason - no one will ever know - a masquerade - hold the door of the cage - seared into the mind - founder on the truth - shall not talk of dread - more than a kindred spirit - fires on the beach - the heart of a diamond.

Oh Mrs. Montgomery. There is little that I can tell you. You wrote the book that contains the whole of my life.

It is such a strange sensation. You are no stranger to Avonlea. You created every flower and every tree.

What have I said that you haven't written? Every feeling I have had has been yours. You invented every thought I have had in my head.

Not one flutter
of the heart
in all her days.

Watching the film of *Anne of Green Gables*. Disappointing, is all I can say – and not because I won't be paid a single dime. New England is not Anne's island. The American flag is not Anne's flag. And Mary Miles Minter, whoever she is, is not my Anne. As I watch the shadows flicker, I thank my lucky stars that Anne is Anne and doesn't have to be me. No movie theatres in Avonlea. Anne will never be tortured by seeing herself on screen.

A publisher who cheats his author out of income.

'How will the world be changed by this war?'– 'How will women be changed by this war?' I sit with my pen in hand and read the questions sent to authors by *Everywoman's World*. Do they know what I will say? – do they know what they want me to say? Do I know what I will say? – do I know what I want to say? There is war in the background of every Shakespeare play. Except the comedies, of course – he wrote those too. There must have been days when he turned his back on the war. I dip my pen in the ink and I write a reply.

He loves his wife and young daughter. He wants them both to be as happy as they can be. He brings the firewood into the home. He lights the oil lamps in the evening. He worries when he hears his young wife cough.

Working on a new novel about Anne.
Calling it *Anne of The Island*.

But can she do it? I wonder. I wonder if she can do what needs to be done. Antony was plain as a plough or a harrow. Antony never had no poetry in his life. His obitchery is the last chance he'll ever have. She says she never really knew much about Antony. All the better for all three of us, I say. I'll tell you the best and you can put it all into rhyme.

To be an actual person - wanders aimlessly - thinking and jotting and thinking - certainly needs a change - swimming for life - a cheerful sobering chat - where is the little boy - look you in the eye - lingering in the neighbourhood - the life that is waiting.

But I can remind you of how I feel. I can recall for you the ending of the book. How you left me on the brink of my future life.

You remember the last few pages. You had me going away to school. You had me studying for a scholarship.

You had me dream of a possible future. Of the beyond of the oncoming years. You had me think of these things with my elbows on the window sill.

People wondered
whether
Az and Za
were twins.

Typing my journal when I am stuck with *Anne of Ingleside*. Sitting here at my window. Letting the rainy days go by. If Anne can turn back and walk through doors then why cannot I? All the past spread out on my desk. I have my pick among pebbles and pearls. Here a tear and there a smile pressed between pages. I lift a moment up and place it in a frame.

A reviewer who has a polemical pen.

Making a plan for *Anne of the Island*. Situation – problem – solution. Lyrical passages now and then. What in the world can I have my Anne be doing now? Wondering how to pay the bills? Pregnant and suffering from the summer heat, as is her creator? It is a long way back to the world of Avonlea. Thinking and jotting and thinking again. I give the morning to Anne and keep the rest of the day for me.

A girl who is afraid she will never grow old.
An author who sees biography as a screaming farce.
A character who talks to her author.

"*The darkest nights.*
The coldest days.

That she would live inside *Anne of Green Gables* forever?
That she would have no other world that she could know?
In the world that you have called your 'world of dreams'?

Ewan's hands tremble at dinner. What is worse is that he doesn't seem to know. A visit to a former parishioner. Unshaven, staring, voiceless – the twin of Ewan when darkness befell him in 1919. Ignoring ghosts as we sleep in our old room in the manse.

Ignore I did
the sunshine.
Ignore I did the light.

One day, the girl discovered an interesting thing.

A pretty good guess - pretty near everything - I must be dreaming - beginning to be afraid - make the roads red - dreamy gaze of a soul - it was only a dream - the whitewashed walls - I've just been imagining - it's been my experience.

A merry little land of butterflies.
Fluffy white clouds blown over frosty stars.
The nights with their sleepy red hunter's moon.

A real poetical obitchery - bat-winged angel - not allowed to see mother - this is your last chance - how such stories get around - how dreams grow - they talked the same language - used to dance and sing - your burned hand healed

- fell off our loft.

The young writer comes to see me. At my house. To empathize with me about my relationship with the CAA. Most of what he conveys is left unsaid. About how powerful is the word of William Arthur Deacon. About how his word can advance or destroy a career. Yes, his stranglehold on mine is quite apparent. I hide the broken ligatures with my string of pearls. Did you wear a disguise when approaching my house? So as not to be seen as fraternizing with the enemy? I appreciate the purpose of your visit. I won't embarrass you with friendly chats at future meetings of the CAA.

A character under the sword of Damocles.

If Frede should die – if Frede should die – while I am gradually bringing a human being to birth. What would I say about life and death? – what would I think and never say? All health to you, my kindred cousin – all health to you, my future daughter or future son. May all of those I love partake of life.

So he went over to talk to the girl. But he hardly got to talk. She went and told him who he was. Then she told him where he lived. Told him everything but why she wasn't a boy.

"The second son is a perfect son."
"You couldn't ask for a better boy than the second son."

They all laugh at me behind my back. They don't realize that I know that they do. Do you know what Mary Maria said, one of them will say each time they need a laugh. Some eat ice-cream at a funeral as a treat. You can dig people up and bury them again. Don't forget to eat everything on your plate. They don't seem to realize that what she says is about themselves. When she talks, she shines a lantern on their lives. Every one of them is living in the dark.

Was mixing with his tears - a fictional home - landing at the dock - looked out through the bars - a story for anne - not know where to begin - the good and the bad thoughts - things that cannot be written - what to leave out - all and sundry.

But think of how I must feel now. You must know how much time has passed. I have no sense of time outside the book.

All I have is what has been written. All I have is what is in print. What is in print and what I sense you will write for me next.

I feel that I am poised. Poised on the brink of my future life. My life is the surf and I am poised to dive right in.

Oh how she wished
that the outside was in

and the inside was out.

There will be life in Ingleside every minute of every day. Not the drama that some might yearn for in the recording of their lives. More like an adventure than a drama, I would say. All the Blythes busy as beavers – or as honeybees in a hive. I am the one who lets the light in. I shift the spotlight from one to the other from time to time.

A reader who always wanted to be an author.

Anne of the Island is coming alive. I count the number of pages each day. A house with laughter and sunshine. A house with only young women allowed. A couple of china dogs to guard the door. Keeping the males at a safe arm's-length. What makes you think you have leave to enter our world? I write in this world in the morning; in the afternoons, I re-enter the world outside.

But there was one thing the little girl got right. She and her brother didn't want to keep a little girl. She and her brother would want to keep a little boy. And she spoke it right out plain. At least you had to admire the gumption of the girl.

Anne of The Island is almost done.
This will be my farewell to my beloved Anne.

The man is walking towards me. It is Matthew – of course it is. He is not very observant – he is not a thinking man. I look at myself through Matthew's eyes. I see a child of eleven. I see an ugly dress. I see two braids of thick, red hair. My face is small and white and thin. There are freckles – freckles galore. My eyes are sometimes grey and sometimes green. I look out at Matthew through them. An elderly man who is walking towards a little girl. If I were sitting on a shelf would I take me home?

You storm-tossed barque - just a dusty red road - too ill to write - sat like a lump - great art is made - was glowing in the woods - a scene repeated - the thorny paths of life - credence of any kind - war in the background.

So what are your plans for your character – Anne? What are your plans for the adult Anne Shirley? What are your plans when I resume my ongoing life?

Will I stay here on the island? Will I take flight to distant shores? Is the whole world open to me as it has been to you?

What has your own life been, Mrs. Montgomery? – if it's not impertinent of me to ask. You were so hopeful when we parted – for sure your life has produced fragrant blooms. Will you flesh out the rest of my life on the bones of your own?

O woe is me.

I don't know what I am.

Oh Violet King – Violet King. You who are starting out on life. You ask me for some writerly advice. You are an Anne without a me – an Anne's-child without an Anne. There is nothing that I can tell you that will be – in the least – worthwhile. If you are not careful, they will eat you – Violet – alive.
A book which barks at everyone who passes.
Another visit to P.E.I. Standing and looking at the old house – walking right through the wall and standing inside. Grandfather sharpening his tongue – Grandmother reading by lantern-light. The pillow flattened where I used to lay my head. Do I dare to reverse the clock? – do I dare to turn back time? Such questions do not occur. I am a very cold-blooded individual – I know a person from a ghost. Pleasant to visit, but I would never live in the past.

"I wonder whether the Reverend has ever thought about writing a book."
"The perfect person to write a biography of his wife."

She was alive

An aunt who stays and stays and stays.
A tyrant who controls the literary scene.
A character who roams around inside a book.

to every nuance

Could you have kept her there forever?
A perpetual life in Avonlea?
A thousand episodes of Anne as a little child?

of the world.

Sometimes I write for money – sometimes I write for myself – sometimes I write for others. Thinking these thoughts while tying a scarf around Ewen's head. Sometimes I work on my novel – sometimes I write in my journal. Sometimes my mind is squeezed so tightly, I cannot write at all.
Writing the last page of the novel, Anne of the Island.
I have finished *Anne of the Island*. I shall soon be forty years old. It was a hard summer's slog. Fending off what must be depression as I am sitting here, day after day, and writing of my Anne – my Anne of the island of everyone's dreams. Into my novel goes the sunshine; into my journal goes the rain. But who would guess when they see me smile? My writing-room is barred to readers – as is most of what's in my head. No red-haired child with freckles and braids am I.

Chapter 6

The new novel will start out with a glance – just a glance – back at the days when Anne was young in Avonlea. When all was bright as a shiny penny found winking in the grass. With a visit to all the places that she found so enchanting in the early days. It will seem to all of her readers – a little less to Anne – as if time in Avonlea has almost stood still.

A sleepless writer puzzling out a thousand details.

Writing a book of poetry. Another visit to the island. Visiting Frede once again. Declining to visit Anne. Ewan Stuart Macdonald – another son – another son. Do the gods work to a plan? Send us a plausible series of gifts? Model the features after my parents? – the shape of the nose! – the glint of the eyes! Glance at the notes they once jotted in haste? 'She already has a daughter – let's send her a son!'

To learn again

A writer who can't think of a story.
A station-master who offers little help.
Two girls having a picnic in a garden.

the meaning

I understand that you get letters?
Letters from as far away as Denmark and Japan?
Isn't it wonderful to have so many fans?

of moon-rise in September.

A sweet song in the heart and on the lips.
Moonlight falling on the orchard.
The murmur and laugh of wood winds.

An old aunt. An old aunt. Why do I think of an old aunt? *Foisted herself upon. Made the children's lives miserable. Scolded and nagged. Insinuated and whined. Blood-poisoning. Rusty nail. Looked with disapproval. A very rare disease.* Yes, I have it now. An aunt who comes to stay and never leaves.

A writer who dredges deep inside her own mind.

So depressed – I feel so depressed. Why do these sudden waves of blackness overcome me? I write books – they sell in great numbers. I am a respected minister's wife. I have two sons – two strapping sons – who will both grow up to have a good life. Why do I sit here in the darkness, after Ewan has gone to bed? The maid knows just enough to leave me alone. The two boys sleep soundly above me. Why is all of this never enough?

So what did the little girl do without a mother? Well, she did what all the other little girls do. She grew up and went to school – learned her ABCs. Ate breakfast and lunch and dinner – played with dolls and grew interested in boys. But there was something – something inside – that was just not there.

"I've never read any of Mrs. Montgomery's poetry."
"I hear she writes it for money for magazines."

I am all alone at the circus! The crowds have left and the music is gone! Sawdust and tinsel cover the floor of the pony ring! Now the bleachers all sit empty! In my ears there is faint applause! Where has everybody gone? High-wire swaying far above me! Smells of sweat and lineament! Just when feeling most alone, I hear a low growl!

List of predicaments - dollops of sunshine - you had me dream - trapped inside a book - a beaten soul - thoughts not-shared - how well do you know - have no life inside - as clear as clear - those who can see.

Anne – I have a dilemma. That is why I so wanted to talk to you. Oh how all those years come back to me.

Years of brightness and kindness and hope. You on the brink of your future life and my life about to change but still quite manageable. I had just finished signing the contract for more books about Anne – about you.

I wondered how to write them. Should I have my Anne grow up or should I write a series of books about Anne as a perpetual child in Avonlea? And now, I have to decide what I should do.

"The more you polish this diamond,
the more it will shine,"
said the one housemaid to the other.

Something happened today that I will never – ever – allow myself to think of – ever again. It is a story that I can never tell to myself. To write it in my journal would be suicide. I must drive it as deep in my mind as the deepest, darkest dream. It will effect every thought I will have for the rest of my life, but I will never think of this happening – not look in its raw, ravenous face – ever again. The cat rubs against me, here in the window seat. My mind is so occupied that I almost forget to breathe.

A publisher who hires an editor to change a book.

A war is raging over half the world. Rolling bandages – weaving shrouds – for the Red Cross. I cannot go to church – I cannot go to the market – I cannot walk down the street – without meeting a woman whose husband, whose son, whose brother, whose fiancé has not been killed or maimed in this diabolical conflagration. The people of Leaskdale are in agony – the only people who are not affected are the people of Avonlea.

He walks behind his young wife's coffin in the procession. He holds his young daughter's hand as they walk along. A tear runs down his cheek as the coffin is lowered. He lifts his daughter up into his strong, warm arms and presses her tiny cheek against his cheek. He holds his daughter's arm as she waves goodby to mommy in the grave.

Writing *Anne of Ingleside*.
Working out a story for Aunt Mary Maria.

All alone beneath the big-top! A cage with metal bars! A cage with growling, angry beasts! Lions, tigers, leopards! One is pawing at the door! The door swings out and stops ajar! I look around but find no keeper! He forgot to lock the cage! The pin in lying fifteen feet away!

Put away in the dark - what is the force - leave to enter our world - borrowed out of books - guess who might be who - a person can be buried alive - so i could better see - provides a little distraction - a fleeting idea - didn't ask him any questions.

Do you know the sword of Damocles, Anne? Did I put it in the book? Well, it means living – existing – with something terrible hanging over one's head – something abominable – which always seems about to drop.

And I don't necessarily mean the physical, Anne – being swept away by flood and field. Well, yes, of course I do – but there are wounds far worse than the physical, my girl. The physical is the least of the lives we lead.

I can't bear the thought of you ever growing up, Anne. The perils that lie in wait for you are frightening to behold. You have no idea what I have suffered since last we talked.

Of course, you have never read my journals – how could you? You could never read my journals unless I put them in your books. And I assure you, Anne – *that* I will never do.

Woe the farmer in the field.
Hit the root and broke the plough.

    Yes, I have it now. She is one of Gilbert's aunts. Aunt Mary Maria will be her name. She comes to stay with the family. Now, what might be the reason she comes to stay? But more important is that she stays and stays and stays. Certainly Gilbert doesn't mind – he is out of the house all day. Family loyalty is strong in Gilbert's clan. So the aunt just seems to stay and stay and stay.
    A reviewer for whom a book is a political statement.
    The war – the war – the war. Ewan refuses to talk about it. Yes, he sits and reads the newspaper, but the words don't explode in his brain. The war is real, Ewan – the war is real. I singe my finger on every village on the map. How can you organize recruitment meetings? – how can you glamourize this war? – how can you justify the news of the dead and the maimed?

A person who constantly goes back and changes the past.
A boy who is good at gymnastics.
A person fiercely protective of her private life.

"*The fading fires.*
The maddening howls.

Fans who read every one of your novels?
Fans who cherish your every word?
Fans who can't wait for you to publish another book?

    Ewan's sermon on Sunday morning at the Leaskdale church. Instead of reading, he speaks extempore. He wanders from topic to topic – lost again on back-country roads. After ten babbling minutes, he turns and sits down. Ewan so calm at the reception – polite smiles from all who shake hands – does he know that he is falling apart at the seams?

Was others stood
outside the wood.
I did ignore them too.

There is the life that is made for us and the life that we get to make.

    Have to go among strangers - sleep sounder at nights - a risky thing - wiser and steadier - could not tell this child - such an interesting world - wandering afar - go on dreaming as long as I could - not to be described in this world - an uncomfortable consciousness - going back to the asylum.

Poplars weaving sorcery of aspen along the path to the barn.
April tiptoeing with sunshine and soft winds.
Village folks hoping for snow for Christmas.

Nearly scalded to death - a badly burned baby - took stock of all - what dovie knew about her - she was a woman possessed - the day of my life - never seemed unhappy or unsatisfied - where nobody heard me - only so much love to give - i haven't any soul.

William Arthur Deacon shrugging into his coat in the coat-room. Surprised to see me shrugging into my rubber galoshes. A chance to say it's quite the winter outside! Well, what is wrong with pleasing readers? Of pleasing thousands instead of pleasing tens? Thousands of readers who know what they like? – tens of readers who must be told? Does he help me with my galoshes? – do I help him with his coat? Our eyes do not meet – we do not exchange one word. Neither one of us suggests we share a ride.

A character who outgrows a particular book.

Frede comes, and we laugh and we sing. The children love her as much as me. We laugh, we eat, we chatter – we go to church and sing the hymns. Even Ewan seems to be normal when Frede is around. Frede is me in my better moments – she is what Anne has been to me. She is Maud without the darkness – L. M. Montgomery without a need for her disguise. She is the person I often wish that I could be.

Told him she wondered if he would come. Told him she would have slept in a tree. Told him she wouldn't have been afraid. Told him the cherry tree was white. And if you thought about it, so were marble halls.

"Does L. M. Montgomery's poetry compare with that of Emily Brontë?"
"Do her poems compare with Emily Dickinson's at all?"

I rush over and close the door of the cage! The panther growls and snarls and frets! His fellows all let out a mighty roar! I hold the door – with one hand – shut! The music starts – the trumpets blare! A miniature parade comes into view! It is the story of my life! Out of order – topsy-turvy – upside-down! My fingers tighten on the door! The beasts are snarling in the cage! The panther's claws slash at my fingers! I squeeze the door with my bleeding hand! With the other, I reach down! I hold the door of the cage as I stretch and strain! With one hand, I try to rearrange my life!

Deeper and faster - a product of necessity - your half of the house - nobody cared about anybody - she was not unique - miles and miles in circles - as tough as an alligator - he sees no signpost - does not make sense - the shadows flicker.

It's just that terrible things can happen to nice people. Even to people as nice as – well, I won't say myself – but to people as nice, Anne, as you. You don't deserve to suffer some of the things that have happened to me.

Who are you and who am I, Anne? That is always in my mind. I took a vow to always keep us completely apart.

Don't you see that I can create another world? A fictional world! – an Anne-world! A world in which only nice things happen to nice people.

I'm having an operation
tomorrow.

The aunt is critical in the extreme. Nothing pleases her at all. She has a comment on every child and every event. She has a spat with Susan, the household servant, if you please. Anne sees the aunt as pouring poison into her dream. Anne is caught between the two. What will Gilbert say to Anne if Anne insists that the aunt must go? I see a crowd of people at a party. Anne is the hostess, with a put-upon smile. The aunt is looking with a grimace of horror at a birthday cake.

A reader for whom a book is a friendly neighbour.

I don't know what it is – I don't know why I cry. Why does Ewan stand so far away? – why do I not bridge the gap? Husband – sons – parish – writing – relatives – friends. Each is no more than a tiny beacon in the night. My life is darkening very quicky. A glimpse of sunlight followed by shade. How many hours of daylight in this part of the world?

A boy would be handy around the farm. Her brother was getting older. A boy would be useful to shoulder the burden of some of the chores. But a girl – what use was a girl? What could possibly be the use of a girl on a farm?

Working away at my story for Aunt Mary Maria.
The dark cloud who stays and stays and stays.

"Look, the CAA should be reserved for serious writers. L. M. Montgomery is certainly not one of those. She is writing entertainment for childish minds. She writes about orphan girls who feel so alone until they get themselves adopted and then all is sunny and fine. So she sells her stuff in the thousands – to readers all over the world. Serious literature cannot be a concoction of sunshine and charm. Lighten up *King Lear* and see what you get. It was an embarrassment to have her on the executive. I organized the vote that swept the old girl out."

Who pays the bills - a cold wind at the door - gems I have sewn in the lining - read them word for word - how naive of people - not unique at all - i have to explain - feels like running away - what I have seen - hide the broken ligatures.

And I could visit you – don't you see? I could visit from time to time. Visit with you as I am doing today.

But, Anne – if our worlds were the same? Where would I go when I need relief? Where would I go when life is too much for me to bear?

What would I do without Avonlea? Where would I go to escape the threat of my Damocles's sword? Your world is the only thing that keeps me from despair.

A violinist and a violin
were the toast of the musical world.
Accolades in a plethora of venues.

Some have said that my books are plot-less. A cluster of anecdotes strung on a thread. A child walking a path on an cloudless day. You are much too fond of purple – just let the sun go up and down. Describe the children and their actions – stay out of their heads. There are two separate worlds in the book-trade: your books are not adult enough for adults and not childish enough for kids. The ink was fine – the paper was fine – but every word of your book was wrong. Well, they should look at the threads more closely. Oh these people who read my books and see nothing at all.

A book which snarls and bites a friendly hand.

Lost in my diary – saved by my journal. Reading the diary – over and over – as the household sleeps. I started writing when I was a child – all my thoughts in ink on a page. Now I read and think again and write again. I keep the settings – I keep the characters – I keep the same or similar events. I keep the dates – I keep the present tense. What I change is what I think – how I feel and what I am. What I am writing about is another kind of me.

"Her poetry is more popular than all those old masterpieces of literature."
"How many people read Dante's *Inferno* or *Paradise Lost*?"

Anne and Maude

A character who wants to write a novel.
A girl whose father died many miles away.
A character who is trapped inside a book.

in a photograph

Do they sometimes feel like jailors?
Do they keep you on a leash?

Do they tell you what to write and what not to write?

with Frede and Diana.

Why is she poison to other people? Why does she go where she isn't wanted? Why does she force herself into other people's lives? Cannot she see how others regard her? Why is she so critical of Anne and her family? Why is she all alone in the world? Why can she not seem to get along with Anne?
An author who stabs himself with his pen.
Leaving Leaskdale – pleasant Leaskdale. Our home for so many years. Where our children were bred and born. Leaving, perhaps, under a tiny misplaced cloud. Changes sought and changes imposed. Both boys will be off to school. Ewan certainly needs a change. We should move closer, I think, to Toronto. There is a life, for me, I think, there. Ewen pulls himself together for one last time. All the ladies speak and thank me. For a moment, I fight back tears. Still, there are many things I shall be glad to leave behind.

Chapter 7

So how many chapters? – yes, how many chapters? Quite impossible to tell at this time. Some characters will have one chapter – perhaps some characters will have two chapters – or even three. Each chapter must have a beginning, a middle and an end. The adventures of Anne – my grown-up Anne – and her Ingleside-brood.
Writing a series of novels in Norval, Ontario.
Arriving in Norval – lovely Norval. A little village with a river – a beautiful church, a red-brick manse. Everyone here seems very cheerful – very welcoming, in fact. We bring no baggage – we carry no bundles. We bring with us nothing of what used to be. We are the new minister and the new wife. Minted freshly as two new coins. Ewan has been chosen – he has been called. Three hundred people struggle through snowdrifts to hear him preach.

To feel

A home with broken shutters and sagging steps.
A maid who does housework all day.
A person mesmerized by a rainbow dance.

sick and cold

Just how well do you know your characters?
Do they talk to you at all?
Besides the dialogue that you write for them in your books?

and empty.

Fields sunning themselves in the afternoon.
A sleigh ride to a Debating Club concert.
Light sifting down through emerald screens.

A mother coming back from a drive. The house lighted up as if it was day.

Where is the little boy who said he would run away? In the outhouse? – in the hayloft? At the harbour? – down at the pond? Where is the little boy who said he would run away?

Writing the first page of the novel, Anne's House of Dreams.

Anne again – Anne again. I hear her knocking on my door. Always another novel for Anne. Oh my Anne is always so demanding. She is the piper who pays the bills. She is the bill-collector who knocks and knocks at my door. Well Anne – my darling Anne – we shall both of us see about that. Am I the writer here or are you? We'll call it *Anne's House of Dreams*; however, we'll see if it's Anne or if it's Maud who calls the tune.

One tries to apply logic to the situation. 'This is wrong.' 'This shouldn't be happening.' 'This does not make sense.' 'This is not the way things were meant to unfold.'

"They've turned Green Gables into a government park."
"It has everything people want to see – except maybe Anne."

Well I've never believed in spiritualism, that's for sure. Never gave it credence of any kind at all. But I'm sure I heard young Walter crying out for me in the night. And whatever did I find? Young Walter on the landing. He should have been at least six miles away. He was crying and cold and hungry. Thought his mother had up and died. Can't tell me that people only talk with words.

My heart is threatening me - think out loud - living in the dark - to print every word - the moon affected her - be an actual person - looking up the latin - not like the other little girls - always re-writing her life - wondered what lay ahead.

You say you have to make a decision. Whether to keep me inside this book. Whether to let the Anne-of-Green-Gables world be my entire life.

Are you asking my advice? Are you giving me a choice? Or are you just taking my opinion into account?

You didn't ask if I wanted to be born. You didn't ask if I wanted to be an orphan. You didn't ask me whether I wanted both parents to die.

So polish it she did.

Ewan's breakdown of 1919 – Ewan's breakdown of 1919. I – don't – want – to – think – about – that. So much thinking was forced upon me when he was crumbling into dust that I vowed that I would never – never – never – ever – think of that time again.

A publisher who takes his author to court.

Rewriting my will. Rewriting my will. Chester in and Chester out. If Chester is father of his family – he is in. If Chester stabs them in the back – why the family is in and Chester is out. So be it. 'Ecce lex'? or 'Ita ratio comparata'? Looking up the Latin for 'It is the law'.

The father was good at many things. He told his daughter about his plans. How aware he was of such golden opportunities. How their little island was a little too small for his dreams. How he longed to make a fortune for her in the West.

Starting a new novel about Anne.
Calling it *Anne's House of Dreams*.

I have never had a friend. Not a drop of love or comfort in old age. There is poison in the wellspring of my life. Bought her a tea-set from Toronto and she turned up her nose. Gilbert admonished me when I said that Di lacked love. Little Shirley called me ugly yesterday. I've tried so hard to be part of this family. All the family wishes me gone. I'll try to think of an excuse so I can leave.

So hard-come-by - a character on the brink - the corpse is me - clinging to the mast - not going well - sweep it from my life - a queen begging pence - all will be well - this is wrong - what is the lesson.

You gave me yearnings but no control. I shudder when I think how I yearned to live here, on this farm. I shudder to think what would have happened if Matthew and Marilla had said 'no'.
And the world of that asylum. And those people at the lumber camp. Did you expect to make merely a mention and let it go?
Those people were very real to me. You created the world I had to live in. You gave every one of those characters control over me.

Woe the fisherman at sea.
Tore the net and lost the catch.

Anne and Diana in the moonlight. Moving smoothly across the page. Dryad's Bubble – Haunted Wood – the Garden – Willowmere. Spring field and ferny wood. A little time in fairyland. Memories of Marilla's red current wine. Childhood, laughter, vows and wishes by the brook.
A reviewer who reserves his praise for his closest friends.
A portrait of a happy marriage. Building a home – having children – making a nest that is warm and safe. Friendship – kindness – love. All of the things that my readers expect. Sitting here at the window – weather changing as the days go by. Making notes for *Anne's House of Dreams*. Dollops of sunshine spread on my pages. Finding a few small drops of darkness seeping in.

A young woman writing a title at the top of a page.
A grinch writing letters in the snow.
An old man who is looking for a little boy.

"What I have seen.
What I have known.

Do they have lives about which you wonder?
Do they give you hints at times?
Do you ever try to peek beyond the veil?

The church at Zephyr – the evening service. Ewan speaks extempore again. He gets lost and wanders aimlessly. Wondering when he will stop and sit down. Scores of people smiling politely and sipping tea.

I hoped the moon
would not be seen
so I could better see.

So she made lives for all of her characters and left their lives at that.

Something that didn't happen often - feel easier in my mind - be in that orphan's shoes - all questions and explanations - glad to be alive - star-led - we're nearly home - call it a good night - pervaded her soul - not even in imagination.

Large winds lashing the maple tops.
A house blooming with firelight and laughter.
A maple tree and a spruce tree intertwined.

A golden hour of a golden day - she slapped bertie's face - there is one consolation - a right to my own knowledge - crumpled up like a child's - marred the afternoon - the wail of the distant ocean - strewn with dead characters - bitten deeply into jem's soul - she is me and i am her.

Sitting by my window. The twilight time of the day. The place and the time where the good and the bad thoughts meet. Wondering how many people I know are truly happy. Let's see. There's one – two – three – perhaps four. No – not four. Definitely not four. Not even three. It's a sad old world with a sad old clientele.
A character who is adopted by the author.
Yes, I recopy my journals. Well 'recopy' is hardly the word. 'Re-fashion'? – 're-configure'? – 're-invent'? 'Reinvent', perhaps, though I'm not quite sure whether this is actually so. 'Re-interpret'? – 're-imagine'? – 're-consider'?

'Re-perceive' – 're-discern'? – 're-constitute'? 'Re-live', I would say. In a certain sense, I relive. What is a life if not lived and relived again and again and again? I pave the road ahead with the bricks I have travelled on.

He never asked her about the orphanage. She told him anyway. Told him he wouldn't understand how bad it was. Nobody wanted you if you were living there. He meant to ask if they'd take her back, but he let it go.

"Now that her husband's retired, they'll probably go back and live on the island."
"She could sell and sign her books every day at the Green Gables park."

The little girl is disappointed. She sees the broken shutters. She sees the sagging steps. I tell her I got sick of living with relations. I tell her I live here on my own. I tell her I'm lonely since Poppa died. Oh, I hope she'll come and visit me. I talk of Poppa and cookies and pigs. It's not enough – I can see it in her eyes.

I can't be sure - such a dreadful feeling - put everything out of my mind - i have saved nicknacks - nothing but complain - meant to record - all we really need - creeps under the door - a few small drops - discovered an interesting thing.

Even Mrs. Spencer's mistake. She sent a girl instead of a boy. Her blunder could have been a cataclysm for me.
She gave me a glimpse of the enchantment of the island. Of trees and fields and flowers. Of marble halls and Shining Lakes and White Ways of Delight.
It was a world of powerful people. They were looking me up and down. I was terrified that they wouldn't let me stay.

*I have a twin growing
inside me.*

Will I have Anne think of the orphanage? Will I have her think out loud? What of the times before Green Gables? When she went hungry – nothing to eat? Should I have Anne recall those terrible days? I see a black creature sitting at a spinning wheel.
A reader who is transported deep inside the self.
Holding the reins of *Anne's House of Dreams*. A strange road and a bumpy ride. A child that is not a child. A marriage that is not a marriage. A man who is not a man. A woman who is not what she seems. Oh what am I doing to Anne – my own, my protected Anne? Who or what is writing this novel? Is the novel writing itself? Who or what is the force that is guiding my hand?

Little girls were smarter than little boys. Always asking why things have to be just so. They would be having flighty thoughts like this one has. Boys would sleep and eat and do their chores. So why would anyone want to raise a little girl?

Anne's House of Dreams is nearing its end.
I shall wave goodbye to Anne at the end of the lane.

We are standing on the platform. Matthew doesn't know what to do. He is wondering whether to keep me or send me away. They asked for a boy – of course they did. Mrs. Spencer has made a mistake. A boy to do the chores around the farm. What should he say to this little girl? He has no idea what he should say. He will let Marilla handle this dreadful chore. Eight miles is a very long drive. He will try not to listen to my chatter. I am talking about the asylum. I have all my worldly goods in this little bag. He wishes I'd be silent and let him think. Marilla and Matthew never have very much to say. My chatter is getting hard for Matthew to resist. He doesn't want to become attached to me.

Assess the damage - my life remains the same - no practical thoughts in his head - you created every event - a closed book - must have been traded - both of us want it to be - worried in the extreme - a character on the brink - by mistake, a girl is sent.

You say you have a choice. I say you have half a choice. You made the first half of that choice when you dipped your pen in the ink and wrote the first words – 'Anne of Green Gables' – at the top of the very first page.
I want life. I want all of life. I will imagine it if you refuse to make it real.
Please, Mrs. Montgomery! – you cannot desert me now! To be an orphan is a terrible thing! No! – you cannot make me an orphan all over again!

One day ,
they found themselves in court.
Perhaps they had been together
for a little too long.

It must be nice to be a Modern. And sneer at everybody's writing but one's own. You and a few of your cohorts. Aim your flashlights in the dankest alleys in town. Write your poems about the refuse and the filth. Call me over if you see anything extremely ugly – I'll shine my little flashlight on it too. Who knows, it might give me a major Modernist poem. Heaps of dismal reveries – dollops of despair. Double-up on *The Waste Land* and win a major prize.
A book which brings smiles to cheerful faces.
Oh, if Anne only knew – oh, if my readers only knew. They all assume that I am Anne if I am any character at all. It never occurs to them that I could be

anyone else. Characters crying out in agony – characters crying out in pain. Characters not in control of their lives – watching the folly of everyone else. I always give myself a part – layered over with a heavy disguise. Only a page or two on stage – raising the drawbridge, spinning the wool. Who would guess the author-character I chose this time?

> "She's created a tourist industry for Prince Edward Island."
> "My daughter wants to get married at the Green Gables park."

The young girl

A woman who suffers from constant nightmares.
A fictional home which becomes a government park.
A person who feels alone at the circus.

dreamed that she

Do your characters make requests?
Do some of them make demands?
Do they ever seek to control the way you write?

would be a writer.

Old sea-captains spinning yarns. A dollar in the hand. The telling of a lie. Wanting a good home. Remote – inaccessible – a stranger. An old deserted house. A bite taken out of the soul. A story for Jem.
Writing the last page of the novel, Anne's House of Dreams.
Finishing *Anne's House of Dreams*. Reading it over with sober thought. What would Anne say about this novel if she could talk? Reading it over, as from a distance. Checking for spelling and not much else. Feeling, now, the need for change – for change after change after change. A new publisher – a new novel, but for sure a novel that is not about my Anne. Too many readers assume I am Anne. Well, I am Maud – I insist I am Maud. Getting the urge to write the story of my life.

Chapter 8

How many pages? – not to be thought of. Much too early for me to tell. A series of episodes in the lives of the Ingleside-people. Of the people of the family – of the people of the community. If each episode is successful — if it is true to its original idea – the number of pages won't be known until I write the last word.

An author's pen moving smoothly across a page.

Oh I take these things – as I have been told to do – but they don't do any good. Whether I take them or I don't take them, my life remains the same. It's like the days of the snake-oil salesmen. All your life will be changed, Mrs. Montgomery, by the magic of just one tiny little pill.

To have

A maid who withdraws to protect her little girl.
A woman whose greatest pleasure is working in her garden.
A driver who refuses to get into a car.

everything seem

Why do you think so ill of the Moderns?
Why do their novels fill you with contempt?
Why do you say they are of the dung-heap and the latrine?

remote and unreal.

Snow crisping under the runners of a sleigh.
The maples behind the orchard turning crimson.
Living in a world where there are white frosts.

A story for Susan. A story for Susan. *The culinary cares. Serene in the knowledge. Captured first prize. Thoughts were her own.* Yes – yes. I have my Susan now. How she keeps the kitchen warm and bakes the bread.

An author for whom writing is a form of therapy.

Chester kisses me again today. The second day in a row. He smiles and wishes that his mom will have a nice day. Chester the actor in full performance – and an amateur one at that. Can't he see that I'm reading his motives – a program with notes as I watch a play. A vase on a flea-market counter, with a crack through the painted heart. Once broken, the vase will never hold water again.

No one's mother should die before they have a chance to know them. No one should have to face their childhood completely alone. No one should have a scrape or a bump and have no mother to show it to. No one should have no memory of childhood lullabies. No one should have to feel so hollow so deep inside.

"So did she ever finally settle with her publisher?"
"They battled it out in court for years and years."

I am a twin! There is another me! She is my sister! She is my friend! But she has no corporeal being! She is trapped in another body! My twin sister is trapped inside of me!

The ring would glow - somewhere in the middle - gently massage my brain - desperate and waving frantically - feel such relief - just down the road from you - give myself a part - true to its original idea - all is agony for me - i take a pledge.

Oh Anne – you ask far too many questions. Why would you care to know anything about my life? Everything I want you to know is in the book.

Anne of Green Gables is your world. It has a cover on the front and on the back. Everything between those covers is yours to love and cherish and enjoy.

Everything outside those covers is not for you to know. And that goes for everyone else in Avonlea. A world with a padlock on the door and freedom inside.

The more she polished the diamond
the more it shone.

Young Mr. Callaghan. At an author's meeting. His novel is being praised as the coming thing. He spent a summer wiping young Hemingway's nose. He is stirring a cup of coffee – I am pouring my cup of tea. So tell me, Mr. Callaghan – I've been wondering what you would say. Does 'Lovers Lane' become 'The Lane of the Latrine'? Eye to eye for a moment or two. He can see that I am not going to blink. He picks up his coffee and turns and walks away.

A publisher who rescues books from oblivion.

Wave after wave of applause washes over me. The Canadian Book Week crowd. A warm and soothing bath for a tired traveller on a cold day. You are applauding Anne – I know you are. That's fine with me – I will take it in her stead. Anne could not be here tonight, as she is trapped between the covers of a book, on a shelf in the public library. I will give her your warmest regards – the next time I go to the library and borrow that book.

And her father wrote her letters. He sent her stacks and stacks of mail. All about his good luck and his fortune. How much fun they would have when he sent for her. All about how he terribly missed his little girl.

Writing *Anne of Ingleside*.
Susan making us both a cup of tea.

My twin sister lives inside me! She eats the food I eat! She breathes the air I breathe! She sees what my eyes see! She thinks no other thoughts but what I think!

Make a dog pretend - merely apple-blossoms - what is the lowest depth - clutching their pennies - wonder who is who - when you break down - so many distractions - a big black dog - a little time in fairyland - among pebbles and pearls.

The book was written when I was a certain age. I was about to leave for a new and distant world. I wanted to capture what life had been like for me to that time.
I was a very sensitive child. Many things had happened to me. Half my life was lived in joy and half in pain.
I took my childhood and split it in half. There was the light and there was the dark. I decided that I would write about the light.

Woe the mother at the cradle.
Kept the faith and lost the child.

Susan filling hot water bottles. Susan in her prize-winning apron. Susan searching the cupboard for a bottle of lineament. Susan giving advice to Anne. Susan baking a cake for Rilla to take to the church. Susan folding the table-cloth. Susan spicing her thoughts with malice. Susan counting the spoons when the ladies have all gone home.
A reviewer who condemns the books of the past.
Ewan knocking over a bookcase. Stumbling around in the thick of the night. A hall-light on and soothing words. It's all right. You're here at home. A little mishap. Soon be right. He addresses a public meeting. Shouting and waving his arms in the hall. How many draughts have you taken Ewan? You should keep track of your intake of pills. Calming him down and back to his

bed. Cleaning the books up in the hall. Well, I'll never get back to sleep. Staying up to write for the rest of the night. Something cheerful for all my readers – let me see.

A farm girl who is played by a movie star.
A person who has more than one name.
A world in which only nice things happen.

"What I have done.
What done to me.

Are your journals sunny and bright?
Do you only write happy things?
Should a good book not be a reflection of one's complete life?

A farewell lunch on Monday morning. Ewan chatting as if he is fine – what could possibly be wrong? His hand keeps trembling as he raises his cup. He doesn't notice as the tea runs down his chin. Ewan smiles and says he will come and preach again.

I cursed the light
and wished it gone.
I only wanted dark.

Never a thought had she for changing a single word.

Know a minute's peace of mind - turning upside down - deeper and more profound - all my worldly goods - rather I didn't talk - couldn't be improved upon - the approaching revelation - the very worst night - such a howling wilderness - as if I were a heroine in a book.

Morning snow weaving its old white spell.
Winds howling along the sand shore.
Good cheer and beds for tired little creatures.

A soul from another star - drowned in a rainwater hogshead - all the trouble i've gone to - went through the ritual - listened to a pack of lies - it's my lot in life - at her own valuation - opened the door in the brick wall - the deadly coils of a python - this was to be her home.

Yes I write – oh Lord do I write. I write of everything that happens to me – bad and worse and worse – every thought I ever have on every single curse. That is all I know how to do – it is the way I am able to think. I think in ink – on a page – in a book. I force myself to think and write it down. Think of a martyr writing his thoughts while boiling in oil – his captors giving him a writing board and his pens and a bottle of ink – the master-torturer saying, 'But don't make a habit of this – if the king gets wind of this, it will cost me my job.' It doesn't make the oil less hot, but it provides a little distraction. Choosing the perfect words while the cauldron bubbles and boils.

A character who is more mature than the author.

There are some things that cannot be written. Not as fiction – not as fact. There are no pages in my novels or in my journals for certain things. Seared into the mind – seared into the heart. An arm singed by a hot poker in the dark. Sleeves rolled down and buttoned tightly – winter cold and summer heat. Into the casket, lid nailed shut and into the grave.

So he took her home in the buggy. Hoped he wouldn't have to talk. Well he got just what he wanted. She told him all about the journey. He had thought he knew all about it, but he was wrong.

"She was tenacious in her suit against L. C. Page."
"He had a passel of high-powered lawyers, but she didn't back down."

I try to will myself to give birth! I squat and grunt and strain! Like the women in the fields of long ago! I want to expel my twin from my body! She deserves to have her own life! She is trapped inside the being that is me!

Sit here in the darkness - force myself to think - the finest things in his life - waiting for her adventure - detects my shaking - snatched from a fiery furnace - just your job - the butter on your bread - under the sword of damacles - what you have become.

So who would live this life? This life that I would capture in a book? This life to be always light and never dark?

And that's where you came in. I needed a girl to sit on the shingles – to talk to Matthew on the ride. To lighten up the world as they drove along.

I dipped my pen in the inkwell. I wrote 'Anne of Green Gables' on the top of the page. And you became the better half of me.

She is the same size as me.
She takes up almost all
the space
in my body and my skull.

Susan pierced by Jem as he tells her she is old. Susan finding Walter shivering on the landing. Susan wondering how to get rid of Gilbert's old aunt. Susan having to hold her tongue. Susan watching Gilbert grow tired and Anne grow old. Susan worried about the state of the tablecloth.

A reader who recoils from a book as from an attack.

Oh these Moderns – oh these Moderns. Bards of the blight of the urban landscape. Peering out through the dirty windows of a streetcar. Writing exquisite squibs on the grime of contemporary life. We co-exist at the authors' meetings. I am denied a breath of fresh air – a short break from my life of toil in the pits below.

And this little girl was not like other little girls. Not that the lady knew any other little girls. Well, she had been a little girl herself – oh so long ago. But the lady, come to think of it, was not like other little girls at all, even when she used to be a little girl. And this little girl seemed even more different than the lady was when she was a little girl.

Working away at my story for Susan.
The anchor of this gently-drifting boat.

"Her husband has caused her a lot of grief. Always bringing things down on her head. He got himself involved in an auto accident one time – with another minister of the cloth, if you can believe. Two old duffers who didn't know where they were going – and they met right smack in the middle of the road. Well, they ended up suing each other. Made all the papers for miles around. Ended up splitting the whole community. Everybody chose a reverend and dug in their heels. The 'who was right' and the 'who was wrong'. Hated each other with Christian fervour. Methodist against Presbyterian; Presbyterian against Methodist. Brother against brother; father against son. In some of the families it practically amounted to civil war. It went on for months and years. Everybody crowding into the courthouse. Taking a turn on the witness stand. Two old duffers who shouldn't be let behind the wheel. What a time her husband gave her. Wasn't the first time – wasn't the last. Their whole life together is quite the merry dance. I'll bet she regrets the day she made her vows."

Stays and stays and stays - a turn on the witness stand - will be self-contained - return to the world - you invented every thought - seems about to drop - perhaps a second diagnosis - cannot hide what you are - in my better moments - starting to realize.

And now I have a contract. A contract to write a book. A whole series of books, if you please.

About a girl whom everyone loves. A girl who sings the joys of childhood. A girl who will live forever in Avonlea.

Readers are clamouring for more. All the world wants to know about Anne. Now – should I give them *Anne* – or give them *me*?

"All the music is in me,"

said the violinist.
"All she ever does is move the strings."

Oh Violet – how can I look you in the eye? You are young – you are a writer – you are me. Still I laugh and chat and smile. Still I give you little tit-bits of advice about your writing. Follow your dreams – never give up – hitch your buggy to your star. A chat with you means two or three days with a heavy heart.
A book which is angrily tossed away.
Oh Ewan – you don't read fiction. You don't know what fiction is. You should take a walk through one of my books someday. There's no telling what you might see. You might see Stuart – you might see Chester. You might see you – you might see me. Will you ever be moved to take a walk some day?

"She didn't get a cent for those Green Gables movies."
"That L. C. Page fellow cheated her of her rights."

Maude and Anne

A writer who creates a tourist-draw.
A woman who pours rain into her journal.
A minister's wife who attends every social event.

in a photograph

Nothing but sunshine in *Anne of Ingleside*?
All lost children will be found?
Not a hint about the grit and grime of your life?

with Maude's parents.

Do some people watch while others live? Are some people servants and nothing else? Do some people have no life inside? Do some do nothing but haul the water and bake the bread? Are some people novels without a story? – are some people stories without a novel? Are some people donkeys going round and round at the mill? Or do they fool us into thinking that they have no life at all?
A writer for whom ink has become a skin-colour.
I am to Anne as Anne is to Susan Baker. Susan Baker is to me as I am to Anne. Anne is to Susan Baker as Anne is to me. And on and on and on. But have I missed something here? What have I missed? Well let me see – let me see – let me see. The butter is on the table. The bread is already sliced. The kettle is just coming to the boil. Well, what do you think, Susan – have we done our quota of thinking for the day?

Chapter 9

Each episode of the novel will be a cell. Each cell will be on its own – each cell will be self-contained. But – drawing back the camera – the reader will see that each cell is only one component of a honey-comb of words – see that honeycomb as the home of all the bees.

A novelist holding a rough draft in her hands.

A night with Ewan in the car. Eight hours to drive a few miles. The car on its side in a ditch. The two of us arguing in the dark. The polite young men who come to help us. Oh, I feel I could die of shame. Ewan crying out to the heavens. Shaking his fist at all the stars. Did such a ridiculous, pettifogging incident give rise to *King Lear*?

To have

A novel mistakenly placed on the children's shelf.
A writer who tells her character what to say.
A woman who is always re-writing her life.

the gold of life

Suppose you wrote an adult novel?
A novel with adult suffering and pain?
Suppose that novel were to be *Anne of Ingleside*?

turn to withered leaves.

Finding out what makes the roads red.
Spruce bows tossing in the night wind.
A purple winter twilight across snowy places.

Now the plan is firm and final. All the old themes rise to the fore. All the bottles scrubbed and sparkling. Vintage wine from what I hope will be a very good year. Anne and her brood and all the trimmings. Send her off on a farewell tour. All eyes look on Anne as she holds her bouquet and waves.

Writing the first page of the novel, Rainbow Valley.
Looking through my notebook. What have I jotted in the past? A hurried thought – a fleeting idea – a magic word. I need to get away from this world – this world of church and home and family. *Rainbow Valley?* – yes, *Rainbow Valley* has an optimistic ring. Perhaps I shall emphasize the children. Perhaps a neighbour will have an arc. I'll keep some distance between myself and my Anne.

But bitterness was not an option for the little girl. She carried on as if her heart was still intact. She had friends among her fellows. She laughed at jokes and sang songs. She went on picnics with sandwiches and a scoop of vanilla ice-cream.

"*Jane Eyre* and *Anne of Green Gables* both start with girls in orphanages."
"That's about the only comparison I could find."

Peter Kirk's funeral. I sit and listen as people speak. My ears burn as the treacle rolls off the tongues. I stand beside the casket. My eyes burn into every face. This ship of lies shall founder on the truth. I have listened as all have spoken. Every speech was a pack of lies. I am the only one here who will say what we all do know.

We travel together - opening up a world - my mind is blank - never held anything back - feel so welcome - reach out beyond myself - walls of glass - take my rightful place - polish it she did - the last few pages.

There's something I've wanted to ask you, Mrs. Montgomery. And that is – how you decide what to put in a book and what to leave out. What to describe in detail – and what to just mention and then pass by.
I can understand that you didn't want to give any details about my life at the orphanage. You have made that pretty clear to me in the past. I agree that it would have been painful to me as well.
But why is there not more detail about my parents? About their life together before I was born. Everything in the book is mine – you have made that clear to me – but I have no access to what you decided not to describe.

The more she polished the diamond
the brighter the diamond shone,
but the diamond got smaller
each time she polished it.

It is not a mask – no, I do not wear a mask. This public face is my actual face. I am cheerful, witty, engaging – I like warm conversations and clever reparté. But people hold a mask in front of me – a bubbly Anne-face on a stick.

They hold it up in front of my face and pretend she is me.
A publisher who publishes authors, not books.
When I leave the house – I cannot go home. When I stay home – I cannot go out. The Nature Club, the CAA – the movie house. All is agony for me. People talk as if they are screaming. Or they whisper what I have to strain to hear. All is agony for me – all is bliss on the silver screen. A ticket for a double-feature for fifteen cents.

And one day the father sent for his little girl. Come live with me in the West. We will hunt and fish and shop and do whatever we want to do. We will have our cake and eat it. There is nothing in the world too good for my little girl.

Working on a new novel about Anne.
Calling it *Rainbow Valley*.

We all sit here making quilts. They don't hear me shout and scream. I am wearing my sumptuous red velvet to a quilting bee. I used to stay in close to the shore. Nobody ever heard me there. I'm too foolish now to dance as the waves burst and tumble at my feet. The bird in the bush can laugh and sing – the bird in the hand is never heard. No one ever seems to hear a word I say.

Ideas fizzle out - give you further life - my bread and butter - won't be the same tomorrow - if all goes well - these darker topics - shall struggle against - the book we wrote together - this dreadful chore - revelling in the world.

Would you, yourself, not enjoy writing about a perfect couple? A couple who were looking forward – with delight – to their first-born child? Would these not have been pleasant thoughts for you as well?
I can imagine scenes from those days. Thanks to you, I have a very powerful imagination. All I have to do to imagine is close my eyes.
I can see the young couple bending over the cradle – taking me, the tiny toddler, for my first walk – showing me the spring-time blossoms on the farm. I can imagine all of this – I can make it seem very real – but it would all have seemed more authentic coming from you.

See the blacksmith mend the coulter.
See the bellows fan the fire.

Boys who argue with their fathers. Boys for whom eight o'clock is bedtime. Boys who hate their maiden aunts. Boys who vow to stay up all night. Servants who snap their tongues at guests. Visiting aunts from Charlottetown.
A reviewer who wants a book which embodies the headlines.
Making plans for *Rainbow Valley*. Episodes finding their shapes on the

page. Troubles for this one – troubles for that. Paint your characters into a corner – why does life sometimes happen this way? – bumps and bruises, but never a wound – never a drop of blood on the floor. Then a clever twist to get them out again. All will be well – all will be well – as all of my readers know. Every reader knows that the ending is guaranteed.

Two ministers who crash their cars on a public road.
A man who suffers from severe depression.
A step-mother who exploits her husband's daughter.

"Let no child
follow me.

Suppose that Jem was lost and not found?
Suppose that Gilbert lost a patient?
Suppose that Anne lost a child in childbirth?

We leave at eleven o'clock at night for our two-hour drive. We argue over which roads to take – every fork and every crossroad – is Toronto this way or that? I get out and read the signpost and insist that Ewan read it as well. He cannot read it – he sees no signpost – he abandons the car and begins to walk. I sit down at the side of the road and burst into tears.

I waited for
the darkness fall.
I plunged into the woods.

But her own life, now, was a tale of a different kind.

As real to me as me - likely to turn out - an uncomfortable feeling - never belonged to anybody - his slower intelligence - when pleasant things end - light being quenched - what good would she be - her big eyes fixed - a grave-yard full of buried hopes.

Lovely rose-colour fields beyond the Glen.
Primroses waking from enchanted sleeps.
The pleasant thoughts of a warm bed.

Anne was herself again - hours of terrified searching - little drama of life - the wings of her imagination - before she knew what he was - so disappointed in ingleside - seems to have bewitched her - some strange land of faery - its rider speared a dragon - am i crazy or are you.

Lonely, lonely, lonely. Ringing up Nora to hear her voice. Talking about a particular day. Spent the whole day at the shore. A picnic lunch and bathing costumes. Not another living creature could be seen. Hid our clothes in a rock and spent the whole day in bathing costumes on the shore. Swimming, laughing, eating and talking – taking pictures and lying in the sun. A lot of talk and a lot of silence – shared-thoughts and thoughts not-shared. We walked home in a fairy landscape – soothing voices in the breeze. The sunset over the harbour – the brilliance of the stars. Both of us knew that we had been given a perfect day. I write of this and paste our pictures on the page.

A character who would like to change the ending.

Do I put everything in my journals? Who would ever want to know? – who would ever be able to know? We are all on stage at every moment – writing the script as we strut and declaim. Not the life, but the presentation of the life, is what we see with strangers, and even with friends. Husbands, wives – children too. Anne presents herself to Gilbert – Gilbert presents himself to Anne. Anne presents herself to her children – of course she does. Why should a journal not be as guarded as everyone else?

He'd thought the island was just the island. Thought the cherry trees were just trees. Thought the roads were just red for no reason. Never wondered how they got red. If she ever found out, he'd be glad if she'd let him know.

"I don't think she's going to be seen as another Brontë."
"The Brontë novels are about the thorny paths of life."

Sitting on the fish-wagon. Selling fish at Ingleside. Jimmy is talking to Nan and her mother on the porch. Nan doesn't look a bit like her mother. Her mother has the same red hair as me. Nan doesn't look at all like her twin. Jimmy beats me when he comes home drunk. My stepmother wishes I wasn't alive. When will I get to take my rightful place?

The least of the lives - suing each other - I have no plans - an ominous sky - every colour of the rainbow - this diabolical conflagration - forged in fairyland - lie awake and daydream - send her out into the world - just who i am.

What is your fondest memory of your childhood, Mrs. Montgomery? What is the nicest thing your father ever said to you?

What is the most interesting thing that you have been told about your mother by those who remember her from the days before she died?

Would these not have been the things – with perhaps a little tweak – that you, as my author, could have given to me?

She is about to be
removed.

Walter in darkness. Walter in fear. How is Walter going to get home? A cold raw wind at the edge of the village. On the road, a big black dog.

A reader for whom a book is a change of life.

Working on *Rainbow Valley*. My world of the paper – my world of the pen. I am spending my time with the children – Jem, Walter, Nan, Di, Shirley and Rilla – Gerald, Faith, Una and Thomas Carlyle. Children and parents – parents and children. I sprinkle them all with their hopes and their dreams. It is raining outside my window. A little darkness creeps under the door. An orphan is facing starvation – what will Anne have to say about that? And now for my ending – now for my ending. Yes – a vision of a piper on a hill.

Her brother seemed to want to keep the little girl. Just like a man to have an idea that made no sense at all. A little girl on a farm would just be an ornament. Her fancy dresses would end up splattered with barnyard manure. If a man ever had a practical thought in his head you could be sure that it was a woman who put it there.

Rainbow Valley is almost ready for the publisher.
Surely this will be my final visit with Anne.

I am with Matthew on the buggy. The steady pace of the sorrel mare. I say not a word as we ride through the village. So afraid – I was – that I would say the very wrong thing. We are driving down a steep hill. Cherry trees and slim white birches. Without thinking, I reach out and break off a branch of wild plum. Matthew doesn't say a word. But now I know what he is thinking. I will have to do the talking for us both. What to say? Oh what to say? That I am sorry I broke the branch? That I would never destroy his trees? Should I keep silent – as Mrs. Spencer told me I should do? Surely one of us should talk. I ask him – again – what he thinks of this beautiful tree.

Don't want to live in a place - your darkest cares - what you want to hear - most formidable fight of my life - every word of the novel - shine my cheerful spotlight - what he conveys is left unsaid - pulls himself together - the bloom might fade - whole world open to me.

So what is a novel, Mrs. Montgomery? I live inside one, but I am not quite sure what it is. What is a novel? – just what does it do?

Is the novel written for the benefit of its characters? Is it written for the benefit of the author alone? Are we good friends or are we good enemies – we two?

You speak of drowning and being saved. Of being adrift on stormy seas. Is the novel doing what you hoped it would do for you?

"*All the music is in me,*"

said the violin.
"All she does is move her fingers and the bow."

William Arthur Deacon – William Arthur Deacon. Arbiter of the taste of the literary crowd. Controlling your corner of that market – reputations attached to your strings. Lists of favourites – lists of foes. A feud for Monday, Tuesday, Wednesday – a feud for every day of the week. Printing your columns in a fiction magazine.

A book which long outlives its author.

I hardly ever see Stuart. It means he is not a burden at all. Always busy with his studies. Shining on the gymnastics team. Two fine oaks – Stuart and I – independent – sturdy and tall. Ewan and Chester – two shrivelled saplings on the forest floor. Able to move along briskly with my novel. White clouds in an untroubled sky. Thoughts of Stuart never cripple my writing at all.

"She should get out and see a little more of life."
"Great novels cannot be written in a parish manse."

One day

A girl who is released by her grandmother's death.
An author who writes a book for just herself.
A war raging over half the world.

the girl created

Suppose that Anne was to die in childbirth?
Six little orphans at the home of the Blythes?
Would it give you six more Anne-of-Green-Gables novels to write?

another girl.

Reading over what I have written. Anne in her old room again. Back in Avonlea for a funeral. No more Blythes in town anymore. Anne as a child and Anne as an adult. Anne with her memories and no double-chin. A cheerful sobering chat with Mrs. Lynde.
Writing the last page of the novel, Rainbow Valley.
The war is over. My book is finished. *Rainbow Valley* is now complete. It allowed me to escape the headlines every day for half a day. Christmas day is tomorrow – will it ever be Christmas again? When a reader opens a book of mine, do they really, truly escape? That – I suppose – depends on what they're escaping from. I wear leg-irons when I walk in Avonlea.

Chapter 10

Gradually, the novel grows of itself – knits itself out of its own entrails. What goes before leads to what happens – what happens is derived from what happened before. Every word becomes a sentence – every sentence becomes a paragraph – every paragraph becomes a chapter. If all goes well with the writing, I just dip my pen in the ink and let myself dream.
A writer busily polishing a final draft.
Success rolls off like drops of water. Failure is the arrow that finds the flesh – the arrow of 'hard to market' – the arrow of 'poetry doesn't sell'. But I am L. M. Montgomery! – with thousands of readers around the world! Only one arrow left in the quiver – it has a label as long as the shaft – 'I am afraid that Anne is you and you are Anne.'

To see

A young writer who asks an older writer for advice.
A person who makes her life a closed book.
A poet who cannot find a publisher.

the colour of

What do they say at the authors' meetings?
'Write about the things you know'?
Why not write about your family or your church?

the meaning of one's life.

A rabbit skipping across a road.
A table set out with the very best china.
Thick scarlet tufts of pigeon berries.

Gilbert has almost had a free ride. At least on the surface of the story. He seems oblivious to almost everything at home. *Worried to death. Couldn't think. Ready to shoot. Come back alive.* Ah – his work. I have it now. A conflict with another doctor. Perhaps a second diagnosis. Something is wrong but the two cannot agree.

A writer for whom writing is merely a day-job.

Ewan Macdonald – Ewan Macdonald. You who lie there on the bed. My life distilled in my journals – yours in a sigh. Have you died and gone to hell? Pitchforks jabbing you as you sleep? Will heaven surprise you when you awake? Angels telling you not to cry? It was only a baddums-dream while you were on earth? Let us hope we are kindred spirits – you and I.

Everyone thought that she was a normal little girl. They were looking at her from the outside. Two eyes, a mouth, a forehead. She laughs and sings like everyone else. There can't be anything wrong with this little girl.

"It's a long way from *Green Gables* to *The Waste Land*."
"It's a long way from *Green Gables* to *King Lear*."

I have a genie in a bottle! It has a cork on top! I take the bottle with me wherever I go! I watch him through the glass! The genie points to himself and then be points at me! He seems to see a connection between we two! What a shame that he has to spend his life in a bottle!

Open up the pages - every blossom on the tree - a rabid quilting bee - i am two people - different kinds of real - just a fact for you - talks of backing out - never tell you a thing - i have a twin - there's a time-limit.

If life goes on, Anne, you will eventually experience all of the things that you so understandably yearn for now. An education, a profession, a place in a community. Perhaps a husband, a child – or perhaps a number of children, we shall see.

But Matthew is gone. Marilla is old. Mrs. Lynde is aging too.

So if life in Avonlea goes on, every one of our people will die of old age too. That is only natural, of course. It certainly wouldn't be your fault, Anne, but if life goes on in the Anne-books, such things would eventually have to happen as a matter of course.

And one day,
when she went to polish the diamond,
there was nothing left of the diamond
but the shine.

Every stone in the road. Every stone and every boulder. Every pothole that gives one's bones a shuddering jounce. Deflating the tires and snapping the axle. Once the mind breaks down, one can never get it safely back on track.

A publisher who never changes a single word.

Oh what are they doing? – what have they done? The Parks Board of Canada – the park at Green Gables. They have torn down the shed where we used to play. They have chopped down the trees in the grove. They will have everything destroyed before too long. The Parks Board is a locust. Green Gables is a tasty morsel in a field of wheat.

Canada is a long, long country. One sits as the train chugs on for days and days. The rock and the trees flew by the window as she wrote and wrote in her diary. She wrote and thought and wrote and thought again. On her way to her dream reunion with her dad.

Writing *Anne of Ingleside*.
Working out a story for Gilbert.

What a shame the genie spends his life in a bottle! What a wonderful life together we two could have! I take the cork out of the bottle and the genie emerges! The genie smiles at me as if there is a connection between we two! He grows and grows and grows – taller and taller and taller! I shrink and shrink and shrink – smaller and smaller and smaller!

Offers little help - trapped in another body - take it day to day - bring no baggage - doctor sighs and shrugs - whether we've met - like working in a mine - what does he need - retreating into the woods - go back on their word.

And you, Anne – after your prime. After the first blush of enjoyment, perhaps. Perhaps earlier than you would think – the bloom might fade.
Not every seedling grows to fruition. Not every dream breaks out into bloom. What you have now can be yours forever – what you hope to have in the future might never come true.
Yes, I have tasted most of life's blessings. Supped at the table and sipped the wine. But I have known bitterness that I hope you shall never know.

See the fisherman sew the netting.
See the needle pull the thread.

Another doctor calls Gilbert in for a consultation. He is baffled by a case. What do you think, Gilbert? What could it possibly be? Hard to tell – hard to tell. Then a lightbulb and a hunch. There's no one in P.E.I. who can save her life. We have to send this lady to Montreal. The other doctor sighs and shrugs. He doesn't expect her to come back alive, but what else to do?
A reviewer who couldn't write to save his life.
Reading a poem to these smug sophisticates. *O, mine enemy!* Parents and friends of the girl Stuart likes. *My lifelong journey!* I don't want to do it, but I can't let Stuart down. *Thine honest hate!* All of my rage is in my elocution.

Scaled such weary heights! They think I'm serving the poem well. *Our mortal strife!* Only Stuart detects my shaking when I am done. He is too young to think of marriage at this time.

A lady who leaves an island that she loves.
An author whose readers know who she is.
A sailor who is clinging to a mast.

"God's gift to man.
Man's twisted blight.

Where does Hemingway get his topics?
Or William Faulkner or Virginia Woolf?
Or Raymond Knister or Morley Callaghan, whom you know?

Ewan driving and muttering and shouting. The wheels are about a foot from the ditch. I keep telling him to move over. He insists that we are fine. Suddenly, the car is on its side.

I never saw
nor ray nor glow.
Was all I saw was dark.

She found she could live her life and live her life again.

Barely visible from the main road - the mysterious creatures - you can't possibly understand - brisk mental processes - has been my experience - grasp the full meaning - lonely, heart-hungry, friendless - unswervingly and unseeingly - what I know about myself - the homeliest baby.

White snowflakes as big as feathers falling thickly.
A harbour sparkling in the golden arms of the hills.
A boy thinking of the beauty of the ripened day.

Anne never told gilbert - distorted imagination - shifted from time to time - tell me a secret - the ruins of her small universe - her heart was broken - days when everything goes wrong - life is a trifle monotonous - regards you as an intruder - this kind of a world.

I throw away as much as I keep. Once, I wrote for over a year and destroyed every word. I want my journals to be published – every agonizing word – so this means that not every word I write can be preserved. Wretched – despondent – anguished – oh I have been all of these. Hideous – hard – terrible – the essence of hell itself. 1919, 1933, 1934 and 1937 – these are the years that slap my face and break my heart. But I want every word to be published – every word I leave behind. So some I write and I destroy and some I write and I preserve. Journal 1 and Journal 2, one might say. Journal 2 will give readers the view of my trail from a distant hill. Journal 1 will be the ashes of my campfire, now grown cold. Not everything I know, but what I want future readers to know of what I know.

A character who grows restless inside a book.

Always questions – always questions. Questions that burn and singe and tear. Every question a burning faggot tossed on the fire. Questions that purify – questions that blacken. Questions that offer a tear or a smile. Do questions ever sigh in regret at what they do?

Told him a few things about the orphanage. How she imagined she had a new dress. A dress as white as the blossoms. Her highest earthly bliss. He didn't see anything wrong with the one she had on.

"How would you compare her books to those of Morley Callaghan?"
"Oil and water, I suppose – or chalk and cheese."

A genie has me in a bottle! It has a cork on top! He takes the bottle with him wherever he goes! He watches me through the glass! I point to the genie and then I point at me! I want him to see a connection between we two! I hope that the genie will let me out of the bottle!

Being out of control - what story do i have - turn to withered leaves - lives can be changed - place it in a frame - maud without the darkness - her dream reunion - deliberately made up a dream - one's complete life - the words kept flowing.

Oh Anne – you can never return to your childhood once you decide to leave it behind. You can never – ever – come back to Avonlea. We shall both be in exile if you decide to leave.

Yes – you hold me hostage, Anne – just as I hold you. As you are my prisoner – so am I yours. Linked together as frolicking angels – chained together as galley slaves – floating on clouds or awash in a turbulent sea.

Should I accede to your request? I *am* the author after all. Why should *I* relinquish the power that is mine?

Consider *my* position, Anne.

You are asking *me* to favour *you* – to favour *you* over *me*. Would you stand upon the shore and watch *me* drown? Would *I* not rescue *you* – in my turn?

The world is a turbulent sea, Anne. Shipwrecked sailors battle the surf. The waves are battering the ship to splinters.

Some are rescued, but many are lost. We cling to each other, Anne, though you are so blissfully unaware. And I am in a position to rescue both you *and* me.

I wonder what will be left
when she is gone?

How many hours difference between P.E.I. and Montreal? Why does that little fact keep slipping Gilbert's mind? The operation should be taking place right about now. Soon he will get a telegram. Do they print the edges in black? Perhaps he should shake off his worries and try to smile for Anne.
A reader who would like to change the final chapter.
Writing a letter to my oldest son. Chester has pushed me right to the edge. I have borne your transgressions with misery. You are both in and out of my will. One last chance – one last chance. Be the son you were meant to be or we shall meet as mother and son no more.

The lady settled down to do some serious thinking. She always tried to think with the head and never the heart. The lady decided not to think of the orphanage. Why think of things that have no practical bearing at all? What does an orphanage have to do with running a farm?

Working away at my story for Gilbert.
The story of a woman who has a chance to live.

"Maud was suffering, I believe. Quite crushed by her ouster from the executive of the CAA. She used to invite me to her home. Told me I shouldn't be seen to be chatting with her at the meetings. The Moderns might purge me from the politburo as they had with her. Very kind to young writers, she was. Encouraging those who were on the way up. Lots of ideas for the CAA. Told me to take her suggestions as my own. 'Nobody listens, any more, to old fogies like me.' Her husband would grunt if he had to talk. I only saw him once or twice. I couldn't tell whether he noticed me at all. She introduced me to him as if he was wallpaper. Didn't seem to expect him to talk. She told me once she kept up with the meetings as a way to get out of the house. Shopping, library, movies – the occasional reading or two. She didn't seem to have other friends. Never mentioned her sons at all. A pretty circumscribed existence. She never talked about money or sales. A quiet person who occasionally smiled. You'd never know she was giving delight to thousands and thousands of readers – the readers of *Anne of Green Gables* who stretched around the world."

In a favourable light - don't seem to quite match - with perhaps a little tweak - thinking was forced upon me - a tyrant who controls - clear the cobwebs - might purge me - brightness and kindness and hope - a world of ink and paper - the reason that I am here.

Oh Anne – you dear, dear girl.

It is a very cruel world, Anne. My own adulthood has had its rewards, yes, but has been filled, pretty much to the brim, Anne, with misery. And you are in such a unique position – I don't believe you are fully aware of just how unique – and how truly desirable – your situation is.

You could be the child, Anne, who remains a perpetual child – a person, in this world of pain, who suffers no pain. Oh, there will be plenty of books for sure – you need not worry about that. In a moment of weakness, I signed a binding-contract – and I must write these Anne-books now, even though I am having regrets, or I will be in a position of one who has broken her word.

Moreover – on top of all my troubles, Anne – I would also be a person who has broken the law. And don't you think old Page would go kindly with me in court – he would have his pound of flesh before the law. No – you are living on a island – an island of sunshine and minor flaws – and you must hug your childhood to you, Anne, and stay just exactly as you are.

Oh my Anne – you are such a child!

Life is too painful for me to bestow on you, Anne! You have no idea what torture is in store for you! I wouldn't wish it on myself, were I to begin my life again, and I would never be able to forgive myself were I to inflict such misery on you – my own dear child!

I have the opportunity to keep you young, Anne, and in a state of childhood wonder, in all of the places that are so enchanting to us both! I have lost that, Anne, but you! – you in your present state! – have the opportunity which is given to no one who is alive! – the opportunity to stay as you are in your happiest, healthiest, kindest, cheer-fullest, most painless days! You can be *you* – with all that is best in you – and *not-you* as well, in the sense that the worst days of your life will never happen to you! Because I will never *imagine* them for you!

On one thing be assured! Life will not come and get you! – life will *not* come and get you! On that I can *guarantee* you can be assured!

Don't you see, Anne? – don't you see? I have nothing in my life to give me hope – nothing in my life to give me kindness – nothing in my life that makes each morning a gift, as it was when I was your age on Prince Edward Island! Oh, I had pains that I thought were pains, but they were nothing to the heartache and the agony with which I have been afflicted in subsequent years! I am Job – with boils on my forehead – in my wretched daily life, but I am Anne in my innermost thoughts, with a young girl's dreams! You are the root on the cliff to which I can cling!

"Let me hear you play together,"
said the judge.
"And when you have done so,

let me hear each of you play
on your own."

Sitting and watching a rainbow dance. A vaudeville stage and a dancing girl. Her dress, as she moves, is clean and white. A magic lantern throws colours on her movements as music plays. Every colour of the rainbow. The colours dance on the white-clad girl. I have never seen anything so beautiful in my life. I close my eyes – I close my eyes. The music is followed by applause. I squeeze my eyes as tight as tight. When she bows, she'll only be a girl in white.

A book after which a reader is never the same.

Burn me at the stake. Pile the faggots higher and higher. Not one soul in the courtyard. Not a soul to see me burn. The royal guard is off on maneuvers – expecting the siege to come from outside. All alone in every endeavour. Not one passerby to lend a hand. I must gather the wood myself and light the match.

"The reason she's not a great writer is that she's had such an easy life."
"People like Virginia Woolf and Joseph Conrad have had great burdens to bear."

Anne and Maude

Two ministers who face each other in court.
A person for whom the past is as painful as the present.
A girl who has always wanted to be a writer.

in a photograph

Why not write about your husband, Ewan?
Your son is Chester, I believe?
Why not write about these people in disguise?

signing books
at the Toronto Exhibition.

Why are people so distracted? Why neglect the loves of their lives? Why are husbands silent partners? Why are wives so prone to worry? Why do we live our lives alone? Why can we seldom diagnose? What operation could cure the ills and stop the pain? Why is everyone thinking what no one else could know?

An author who writes great books which never sell.

Leaving Norval – pleasant Norval. Our home for so many years. Leaving, once again, under a tiny little cloud. People are so tolerant of what they cannot possibly know. Kind to me – kind to Ewan – wondering what in the world we are. Released from bonds that drove me crazy – released from bonds that kept me sane. And Ewan – amazing Ewan – the black and white bear I keep in a cage. You earned your keep with a weekly sermon – tea and cookies every Sunday after church. Prometheus and Mrs. Prometheus – released from our chains, at last, on the rock. We can go anywhere in the world – now where shall we go?

Chapter 11

The ink flows across the page. The novel moves along. Deeper and faster as it finds its natural course. Many drops form a river – many rivers form a sea. Now is turmoil – now is calm. The reader struggles – the reader relaxes. The reader is a paddler in a canoe.
Writing a series of novels in Swansea, Ontario.
Moving to Swansea – lovely Swansea. Such a snug little town. A home of our own after living so long in a manse. A new home with a view out over the lake. We can watch the storm-clouds gather while safe inside. And Ewan – you storm-tossed barque. Here you can hide – here you can hide. You can hide inside your countenance. Quiet mornings and afternoons. Pleasant chats with casual acquaintances. When you break down, we can hastily close the doors. And I shall take the trolley to Yonge Street to shop. I shall enjoy the monthly meetings of the CAA.

To be

A child who is born with her skin inside-out.
A writer who is unwelcome in a writers' group.
A man on the right road who feels he is lost.

a woman

What made you decide to keep a journal?
What would you say that a journal is meant to record?
Is such a journal meant for you and for no one else?

with an excellent chance of living.

The deep blue water of the St. Lawrence Gulf.
The path up the spruce hill to the school.
A girl with her arms full of gorgeous boughs.

Oh Anne – oh Anne – oh Anne. Child of my reveries – child of my dreams. Child of my bumps and bruises. Child of my fears – with a lighter touch. At times you try to be the parent. With a parent's firmness, I gently turn you down. What would our lives have been like if you had invented me?

Writing the first page of the novel, Rilla of Ingleside.

I do so love this house. Someone asked me – when we moved in here – whether it could possibly rival Green Gables. Why yes, I said – it has running water and the street is paved.

So a mother dies of tuberculosis. Terrible things have happened before. People die like flies in plagues. Earthquakes open up and swallow villages whole. The little girl was not unique at all.

"Does Mrs. Montgomery sometimes seem distracted to you?"
"Once in a while you catch a tiny glint of sadness in her eyes."

The boy's father died. Then his mother died. His aunt wouldn't let him keep the dog. Jem bought the boy's dog for a dollar. Jem sits and mopes; the dog sighs and mopes. It's clear that the dog will never forget the boy and learn to love Jem. You can do a lot for children. Bake cookies and two kinds of cake. What you can't do is make a dog pretend.

To learn again - a chance to know them - i live inside a book - give me further life - if life goes on - what you don't dare say - when you were optimistic - what is best for both of us - i already have a title - the state of my life.

I wander around inside the novel. In every corridor I find a series of locked doors. Sometimes it almost seems that I, too, am confined.

You put my mother and father – dying – in the novel, Mrs. Montgomery. It might have been just a fact for you – just a mention in just a few words – but it was very real to me the moment it was written down. But why can I only find just those very few words?

Why are these darker topics not dealt with? Why are they mentioned and then not explored? I have to assume that you included these things for the character – for me, Anne Shirley – and I also assume that you included them for you.

Two people inherited a house.
An elderly person had died.
An elderly uncle, perhaps,
or an elderly aunt.
I can't be sure.

Oh to be tepid and mundane. Oh to be at home in this world. Oh to be able to write of the life that one actually lives. Of the latrine and the pile of dung. Of the squabbles and petty spites. Of the boring – of the dull – of the everyday. A prize for the novel which puts the most readers to sleep.

A publisher who is contributing to the culture.

Being interviewed for a story. The accomplished author of *Anne of Green Gables*. She is so cheerful and amusing, as one would expect such a writer to be. Her husband sits beside her and nods at her every word. So is there a new Anne-novel in the offing? Yes, there is – there certainly is. Anne and I are close companions – we travel together – together through life. I plan to call it, *Rilla of Ingleside*. A smiling mouse in the jaws of the family cat.

Her father was a very important man. He was often away from home. The Canadian West is a very large place. He had to travel for miles and days. She would sit by the door and wait for her father to come home.

Starting a new novel about Anne.
Calling it *Rilla of Ingleside*.

That woman is never happy. She doesn't belong in this family. She must have been traded with another aunt at birth. She cried when she was told not to talk of red hair. She cried when she was told not to prune the spirea. She sobbed when she was given her birthday cake. She doesn't deserve a birthday party. 'Withdraw thy foot from thy neighour's house.' It's better she take her poison somewhere else.

Forgot to lock the cage - shivering on the landing - hand on heart and eye to eye - opened his eyes - a pretty circumscribed existence - can never tell to myself - i fumble with the door - wander around inside - another kind of maud - wouldn't expect to control.

Authors should be aware, Mrs. Montgomery, of their responsibilities. Once you create a character – once you write the final word of a book – why then you give up all control. The characters are free – or condemned – to live and think – yes, and feel – inside that world.

If you didn't want me to think of these things, Mrs. Montgomery, you shouldn't have put them in the book. Don't forget, you gave me imagination too. Yes, I think about my parents – though you chose not to write about them.

You can't include dying parents in a novel and assume that they won't be seen. Whether you think you have or not, you have opened up the pages and let darkness in. And I thank you, Mrs. Montgomery – I thank you.

The little fisher-girl
sits with her parents
at a stall in the market.

Anne on the train – going home. A joyous house – a proper home. Home to Ingleside and Gilbert and the brood. A cat with its tail bitten out at the root – a child standing under a horse – a kitten tortured in the village and brought home. Anne of Green Gables for a week – Anne of Ingleside for all the time to come.

A reviewer whose pen has buried many a book.

Working on the plot of *Rilla of Ingleside*. Why do ideas not come forth? I have Anne – I always have Anne – but she resists sometimes when I move her around on the board. Nine months of jottings and scribbles. Shall I have her do this? – shall I have her do that? Ideas fizzle out on the page. No, my Anne is not an actress. She will not take a role in a play. It must be the actual life of Anne or nothing at all. Anne always knows what is Anne and what is not Anne.

A writer who fights for damages in court.
A boat of precious cargo bound for the rocks.
An author who is cheated of movie rights.

"I cannot tell.
I cannot tell.

Have you written what you don't dare say in public?
Have you written thoughts that your novels don't contain?
Would you say that you have led two separate lives?

Ewan is slumped against me. He has no idea where we are. I reach back and retrieve my suitcase. I give Ewan a shot of brandy to calm him down. I get out and assess the damage. Engine running – lights burning – we'll need help to fix this tire.

No lantern brought I
to the wood
I did not want its glow.

So she thought her life and lived it over again.

Built at the farthest edge - his heart troubles him - the tense rigidity - worse than anything - been one of my dreams - the dark blue gulf beyond - the most tragical thing - cried herself to sleep - her spirit was far away - stick to bald facts.

A little dryad who comes out at night and talks.
Big bumble bees booming over the nasturtiums.
A little village fringed with icicles.

Didn't belong in my own home - spared a lot of trouble - a temporary confidante - this is the truth about you - blind, crushed, despairing - little baby was born dead - didn't think it meant anything - another summer was ended - what a butterfly hatches out of - i'm so glad i'm me.

Yes, I write to a number of people. No, I won't tell you who they are. The two of whom I am thinking are both male and about my age. I have written to them for years and years and years. Whether we've met is completely irrelevant. Merely a moment – pleasant or not – to be endured. No – it's not them – these men – who are interesting. It is me that I want to explore. What I say and what I don't say – what I put in and what I leave out. What I alter – slightly – in the telling. What I think but don't write down. I barely read these men's replies. My letters to them I read again and again and again.

A character who is blessed with imagination.

I want every word that I have written to be published. Every word of every journal at which I have toiled. Every heartbreak on every page. Every blister, cyst and boil. Anne I have snatched from a fiery furnace. Peel the bandages from my skin and show the scars.

He kept thinking about the asylum. Four months is a long, long time. She would lie awake and daydream. That was how the girl got along. She would lie awake and imagine all kinds of things.

"She's always so bright and cheerful when you meet her."
"The perfect woman to be a minister's wife."

What could Anne have been? She could have been a writer. She used to write such clever little things. What could I have been? I could have been an Anne. I could have married Gilbert and raised a brood. What does the mirror want to say? What does the mirror want to know? Why does the mirror always judge but never talk?

Polish and revise - always felt like rain - we are all on stage - knocks at my door - spoke it right out plain - far from shore - offer a tear or a smile - yes, I have it now - an ox attached to a wheel - strains at its tether.

When you included these dark moments in your novel – in *our* novel – what did it mean? Why did you include them among the stories? I have to assume that it was very important to you.

You cannot hide what you know. You cannot hide what you are. You seem to see yourself as the darker half of me.

To live in sunlight every moment would be to have no life at all. It would be a life with no connection to you. If you think of me as your life-line – as you have told me in the past – then think of you as my life-line too.

The ship was just off-shore.
A St. Bernard could have swum to it in about ten minutes flat.
But nothing could survive in that raging sea.

Working for hours and hours each day. Occasionally taking a break to deal with a Ewan-spell. Ranting and raving fit to be tied. Chucking his medicines in the garbage. Vowing to touch them never again. An hour later, asking what I have done with his pills. Pick a doctor to please yourself. Doctor One says dig in and bear it – Ewan will never be well again. Doctor Two says he'll soon be fine with the help of these pills. I calm Ewan down and get back to my writing. I've carried an elephant on my back for nineteen years.
A reader for whom a good book has no author.
Sometimes novels write themselves. They guide the pen across the page. All the writer is able to do is read the words. The children are taking over the picture. Rilla is pushing Anne aside. It is the children who are going off to war. What does Anne think of this novel? She waits in the wings for her scene to start. Oh I am sorry, Anne – I am sorry. Rilla has taken the pen from my hand. The piper's tunes are growing darker. The edge of a dress is getting wet from the blood-red tide. I seize the pen and write an ending for Anne and I.

Mind you, the girl wasn't quite so flighty as she might at first appear. She had figured out the whole situation at a glance. There was a bluntness that, to the lady, had an appeal. Now if someone could make the little girl a little less flighty, and a little more down to earth, that someone might be rescuing the girl from a life of ridiculous thoughts. Her brother was right that someone could do some good for this girl.

Working diligently on *Rilla of Ingleside*.
Rilla is almost pushing my Anne aside.

In my hand I hold a tiny branch of wild plum. I am on Prince Edward Island. The prettiest place on earth. I close my eyes and picture trees. A house with trees all around. And little mosses and Junebells growing over roots. There is a brook and birds are singing in the trees. Matthew is thinking that he likes me. He hopes that I can stay. He is worried about Marilla. She never wanted a little girl. She will say they want a boy to do the chores. Yes, I know what Matthew is thinking. Matthew likes to hear me talk. I tell him my highest ideal of earthly bliss.

That kind of writer - an inner glow - get out of this dream - sees the broken shutters - put everyone in the spotlight - lived and thought and lived again - seeing herself on screen - lighten up king lear - she never shared - miss my old vantage point.

Well – just let me be myself – Anne Shirley. Whatever she might be. And let the chips – or the Damocles's swords – fall where they may.

That is all a character expects of an author. At least a character like me. And you created me – so, whatever I am – whatever I want – whatever I imagine – whatever I demand – is an echo, in a very real sense, of the essence of you.

I want to see more of life than I have so far. I want the sides of this novel of ours to open out onto the big wide wonderful world. You seem to have made me more adventurous than you seem to want me – at this stage of your life, at least – to be.

But wait – don't go just yet, Mrs. Montgomery! – there is more that I want to say!

The death of Matthew – my stay in the orphanage – the deaths of my parents! You have put them in the book! You cannot go back and write them out again!

Doesn't everybody get to have a full life? Why can I not go out into the world? – why can I not experience the joys of all of the stages of encountering life and making it work? I can deal with any crisis just as you have done in your life and as everyone has done since time began!

Will I die in childbirth? Is that what you plan to write about? Or will I just have temporary pain – and a glorious birth – perhaps with twins – and be the best mother to them that a mother can possibly be?

Everyone has dreams.
Have you noticed?

We can manufacture dreams. We can dream a dream out-loud as it were, at the very top of our minds. I did it deliberately today. We were driving home from Peterborough. Ewan and I took the old roads we used to know. So I deliberately made up a dream – a dream of before 1919 – a dream of that moment from a distance of twenty years. Before Ewan went off the rails – broken Ewan, who sat beside me driving the car. I imagined myself coming home from Toronto – just as young as I ever was. Two rosy lads with shouts of welcome. Ewan himself, wholesome and cheerful – dimple-cheeked and a jolly smile. The smashed vase as it was when I bought it – not broken at all. Then we all went inside and sat by the cosy fire. Life would go on this way for ever and ever – I knew, I knew, I knew. A little bump in the road I, suppose, and the bitter present returned. Then I tossed the dream aside with a bitter smile. Ewan, of course, never knew what I was thinking as we drove along.

A book which seeks out its ideal reader.

A word or two on my family history. The people who made me what I am.

A very nice crowd and a nice introduction. So nice to meet my readers face to face. The Montgomerys of Prince Edward Island. Scottish roots and Canadian crops. Montgomery's tavern – muskets and pitchforks – I have roots in Toronto too. Turning the apples to hide the scabs. Some people bring Anne to have me sign her. A gentle lady asks me to say hello to Anne.

"She always seems to be just another person."
"Not my idea of an author of famous books."

A girl

Two people arguing in the dark.
A man walking behind his young wife's coffin.
A swimming-bladder bobbing on the waves.

almost as real

Are there gaps where you decided not to record your thoughts?
Are there things about which you feel it's too painful to write?
How faithful, then, is this record that you will leave?

as was the girl.

Walter creeping in the darkness. Heaven a million miles away. Susan turning on her pillow. Is that Walter's voice she hears? Susan searching the darkness – flannel nightdress – ears alert.
Writing the last page of the novel, Rilla of Ingleside.
Rilla of Ingleside has ended. The novel was wrested from my hand. Who am I when I am writing? – am I Rilla or am I Anne? I don't know who commands my pen any more. I write a dedication – to Frede – to Frede my own true friend. Should I have written the dedication to my Anne?

Chapter 12

Characters learn to live in a novel. Jostle at the feed-bowl – stake their turf. Learn to sense their contribution to the whole. They cry out for proper placement – place me last! – place me first! I see myself at centre stage! – I see this novel as the story of my life!

An author submitting a manuscript to a publisher.

Tossing and turning on my pillow. Dreaming of being out of control. Waking up as the dream is fading. Waking up and finding the dream is all too true. A boat drifting out of the harbour. All of its cargo bound for the rocks. If I were still dreaming, I could swim out and salvage the wreck.

To be

A woman desperately holding a cage door.
A young girl who feels another has taken her place.
A dreamer who dreams of being out of control.

a released bird

Why have you asked your son to publish your journals?
Why have you asked him to wait until you are dead?
Why have you asked him to print every word?

flying again.

The tinkles of sleigh bells and distant laughter.
A crisp September morning on the Birch Path.
The great shimmering sparkle of an evening star.

And what of Anne? What story of Anne? What story of Anne at the ending of *Anne of Ingleside*? *Not getting much fun. A piece of furniture. Severe attack of lumbago. Under the harrow. Heart had been wholly buried.* I see it now. I see it clearly. Darling Anne – feeling old – darling Anne will feel herself to be under attack.

An author who falls into an inkwell and can't get out.

Frede of the days of my youth. Eye to eye and mind to mind. The perfect words for every occasion – every eventuality. Everything that came our way would glow with words. All of them borrowed out of the books – borrowed and polished and never returned. I dreamed that I could make myself into a book.

But the little girl was cursed with imagination. She was sensitive to all things in the extreme. She felt every single raindrop that fell on her skin. So loneliness was, to her, like being in prison. She looked out through the bars on the human scene.

"The purpose of literature is not to make us feel depressed."
"The purpose of literature is to present a splendid ideal."

It looks like a child's head on a swimming-bladder – bobbing and wind-blown – far from shore! Waves are tumbling as I plunge in and start to swim! The head bobs up and then disappears and then rises again and again! I swim towards the struggler with all deliberate speed! A wave surges and the head is lost to me and the wave subsides and I catch a glimpse again!

Its raw, ravenous face - to lighten up the world - the story of your life - not of oneself, exactly - accede to your request - i have a dilemma - exhausted and terribly sad - my bumps and bruises - situation 1, situation 2, situation 3 - you lurk inside me.

They say we dream away our lives. They say we dream and dream and dream. Most people seem to be unaware of their dreams.

But I am always in touch with my dreams. And – God forbid – with my nightmares too. And writers – as you know – make books of dreams.

Sometimes I dream I am other people. I have been everyone I know. What happens when other people dream of me?

The two sat and listened
at the reading of the will.
They were siblings, perhaps.
Or perhaps they were distant cousins.
I can't be sure.

Oh Violet King – Violet King. The pen will up and bite you. The page will take you by the throat. The ink will drown you – many times over. You are me – Violet – the me of 1905. Even your characters will turn against you. Your finest creations will have your head. Readers will chant in praise as the platter is shown around.

A publisher who is providing a variety of voice.

Sitting here at the authors' meeting. More life in a quilting bee. Rise about ten o'clock in the morning. Yawns and a headache from the night before. Put the kettle on for coffee. Clear the cobwebs from the brow. Scribble your gems on scraps of paper. 'The sewer rats are wearing spats.' 'The old man's horse is in the bourse.' Knock off at three and walk to the bar. Drink and talk the night away with fellow bards.

The father had a new wife. He had married a second time. Why remarry when you are often so far from home? Why leave your little girl to live with strangers? She would sit and wait for her father to come home.

Writing *Anne of Ingleside.*
Working out a story for Anne.

I am tired but I am determined! I am swimming as fast as I can! The struggler must be exhausted! I swim up and down the waves! I can't believe that the head keeps bobbing up again! I am far beyond the shore! The wind is attaining ferocious speed! The poor soul is drifting out to sea!

Our eyes do not meet - a cause of pain - the gold of life - your monumental feat - you had me think - ten babbling minutes - will have everything destroyed - the essence of you - everything outside those covers - you don't bring it home.

You know, I have always been called just 'Maud'. Never 'Lucy' nor 'Lucy Maud'. For the books, I chose 'L. M. Montgomery' as my name.

I chose your name very carefully, Anne. A name is one thing about which Juliet is totally and completely wrong. There *is* something in a name, don't you think?

At readings, I sign my books. I sign cheques all the time. Sometimes I catch myself signing my name with an 'e'.

The little farmer-boy
sits at a stall
in the market
too.

Darling Anne is under attack. The boys' pup. Susan's blanket. Nan's new kitten. Pounding drums. Rilla's earache. Shirley's rash. Getting ready for an occasion – the anniversary of Anne and Gilbert's wedding day. Gilbert whose dinner-talk is of measles in Upper Glen.

A reviewer who is envious of a writer's skill.

Well, I always plan. Plan – plan – plan. I cannot write a novel unless I plan. I plan – and then I write – and then I polish and revise. So where is the spark? – where is the magic? There is magic at every step along the way. If I am not Anne, I cannot write Anne. If I am not Jem, I cannot write Jem. Do you see what I mean? Oh yes, I see the twinkle in your eye. You are going to ask if I am Bruno when I am writing of Bruno and Jem. Well I am Bruno and Jem and Robbie Crawford as well. I couldn't write the book at all if I were just me.

A procession of black coats and black hats.
A husband who suffers a nervous collapse.
An actor taking a bow as the cock crows.

"*Seal up the path*
where I have trod.
Let no one
trace my steps.

Do you not feel that your son loves his mother?
Do you not feel that he might prefer you to be remembered in a favourable light?
What if he hesitates to print what you have written?

On the road at two a.m. Ewan driving too close to the ditch. He keeps insisting that he knows how to drive a car. In the distance some oncoming headlights. As Ewan pulls over, we are in the ditch again.

Was thrashing through
the underbrush.
Was searching
high and low.

Then she thought and lived and thought and lived again.

Can get used to anything - received a severe mental jolt - scope for imagination - lie awake at nights - pretty nearly perfectly happy - a white-clad girl - investigate this affair - a flood of cheery sunshine - the wings of imagination - when were you born.

Blueberry bushes turned scarlet.
Knightly hollyhocks against the brick wall.
A dragon guarding a stone bridge across a brook.

Should be blight not blythe - surged up and overwhelmed him - nobody but happy people - being banged about - this horrible knowledge - told the truth about him - one of those peevish creatures - would be children no more - the time to bargain with god - tell the gold from the tinsel - her rightful place.

Another letter from Saskatchewan. My, how his life has shrivelled and shrunk. We started out together with all of life a climbable hill. Teaching school in rural Saskatchewan – what did he think that life would be? Teaching school at Buckingham Palace? – adopted as prince when you catch the King's eye? – teaching everyone in the kingdom their ABCs? With every letter, he makes himself smaller – the petty cares of petty days. So, why do I heed the mail-man's ring? O Damocles, my Damocles – you are sitting in my stead – a letter-opener hovering constantly over our throne.

A character who is cursed with imagination.

Ewan never thinks of money. Why should he, when manna falls from the sky? He loves his cakes and pies – his vegetables and gravy and roast beef. Does he realize that we would starve to death on his salary? I wrote for money when I was a girl – I write for money now. It is Anne – not Ewan – who pays the bills.

She would imagine she wasn't so skinny. She would imagine she had some parents. She would imagine she was a bride. She would imagine some evil nurse who up and died. He hoped she wouldn't imagine they'd wanted a boy.

"The greatest books are the ones that sell millions of copies."
"What's the point of writing great books if they sit on a shelf?"

I wipe my eyes and try to focus! Perhaps it is only a child's ball, ducking and drifting on the waves! But how can it not be a person? Did I not clearly see it wave! Surely I saw it waving! It was desperate and waving frantically at me! I move my exhausted body! I was the only one on the beach! This cannot be just an illusion! I'll never forgive myself if I let this poor child drown!

Pursued by what - a person who feels trapped - balloon has drifted to earth - making a nest - they make me weep - in the ditch again - orphaned your own mother - possibly be the use - as plain as day - the storm-clouds gather.

But Anne – my Anne – what could you propose to write that I haven't already given you to write? I have given you the best of my own ideas. I have given you my emotions and my thoughts.

You have described Avonlea in a way that so many readers have come to love. The Shining Lake – the White Way of Delight – the people and the events. In all those passages that I wrote for you to say.

I could make you a writer of poems – of the earth and of the sky. Landscape poetry, it is called in the trade. There are poems of that nature in magazines.

But Anne! – oh Anne!

No! – not the orphanage! Surely you don't wish to write about the orphanage! The orphanage will be there – it will be mentioned in every book – but it will *not* be written about!

We are not that kind of writer, Anne! That is – neither you nor I! We do not wallow in the filth and the mire!

What I have lived has been so very painful! Take my word – it would be agony to you! If these Moderns had lived my life – they would be silent on the gravest topics too!

The ship had hit a reef.
The waves were breaking it apart.
You could see the sailor clinging to the mast.

Darling Anne is under attack. Other women seem so much younger. Christine Stewart from so long ago – the lady who has the secret of immortal youth. Why has she not kept up with her writing? What was Gilbert's choice of wives? Why bring so many children into the world? And Gilbert – wonderful Gilbert. Gilbert who has no gift for Anne. What is eating at his heart? What is gnawing at the core of their daily lives?

A reader who is disappointed in a book.

The Young People's Christmas Pageant. Chester bulls his way into the cast. All of the drama is in the rehearsals. Chester's bluster elicits sighs from all the young girls. What are his children doing while Chester flirts with the cast? Chester denies his master thrice. As the cock crows, he takes a sweeping bow.

The lady tried to ignore what the girl had said. That there was no life for her in the orphanage. That nobody cared about anybody there. That they didn't even send the girl to school. The lady was trying not to read between the lines.

Working away at my story for Anne.
Barely recognizing her in her fortieth year.

"Yeah, I was called out to fix a tire for them. Mrs. Montgomery and her husband. It was a terrible rainy night. Dark as pitch out on the highway. Got a phone call from someone who lives on that road. Was Mrs. Montgomery who came to the door, I was told. Her husband just sat like a lump the whole time in the car. Well – not when I was there. Here I am taking off the tire and trying to put on a patch – in the pouring rain, mind you – and the husband up and shouts that he's being pursued. Pursued by what, I wondered. Anyway, here it is pouring rain and Mrs. Montgomery is off in the dark, calling out to her husband to come back and get in the car. So I offers to help her out – he was a little ways down the road – but she says 'No, you fix the tire. I'm fine on my own.' Well – a nightmare if there ever was one. I got the flat all patched and pumped her up and put the tire back on. Then she gets him in the car and he don't want to drive. I assumed she didn't know how to drive so she's coaxing him. She told me they'd started off from Leaskdale at eleven o'clock. That's just a little ways down the road. They shoulda been home in about two hours and here the clock was pushing six – six a.m.! Anyways, off they goes. And the next time I seen them was when I went to their church. I had a niece that was being baptized and I said hello. The husband said hello and all. If there was anything wrong with him you'd never know. Mrs. Montgomery was polite but that was all."

Rows of little puppets - could I help you - like a character in a book - a dollar in the hand - the unpleasant reality - a sullen pot of lead - have no other world - changes sought and changes imposed - to polish the diamond - all of my rage.

Oh my Anne – you are so naive!

All of these people – Mark Twain, for heaven's sake! – are not praising the novels that I might someday go on to write, my darling Anne! They are praising the little girl they love when they read about *you!* They don't want mud and blood and gore!

They don't want the agony that I have endured! They don't want breakdown and decay – and their dreams all smashed in pieces on the kitchen floor! They want *you!* – more of *you!* – they don't want *me!*

Oh Anne, I am begging you – do not condemn me to only the pain of my days – give me the dreams of my nights! Give me the moments of bliss that make bearable the pain of the hour! I gave you life! – now give back life to me!

Oh Anne! – for heaven's sake, Anne!

Have you considered the danger of marrying a man who might turn out to be a burden and a detriment? – a dolt and a drudge? – a dotard? – a man who is lost in life? – a man without a core? Of bearing children who might turn out to be a worry and a curse? – of terrifying social events such as war and depression and world-famine? Oh Anne! – oh my Anne! – whatever profession you might see as your life's work might be trivialized and stigmatized by snobs and oafs and the thickest dunderheads!

Would you want such a life as the Moderns would give you? These Callaghans and these Knisters? – these Eliots and these Woolfs? They set their stories in the foul latrines of life!

I give you life and you complain that it's insufficient! Shakespeare is oh so right in what he observes! 'Sharper than a dragon's tooth is an ungrateful child.'!

Some have two or three.

I read over some pages of my first diary today. Pages from almost sixty years ago. In the year 1892, I wrote a line that I have not written since: 'This year has been a very happy year.' Many people who were woven into that year are now long dead – many people who are part of my life came along many years later. Time controls us and we control time – life makes us and we make life. There is the year and what I wrote about the year. I can't go back in time, but I can go back and rewrite my diaries. This is one line that I have decided not to rewrite.

A book which guards the reader like a dog.

Polite applause at the ladies' Book Club. What do you see when you look at me? You who are here to enjoy my little talk about myself? The dreamy author sitting at the window, waving to her character, with Anne waving back on her way to school? The Canadian author – rare bird – who is read by dreamy readers around the world? Perhaps I'm the grunting hunch-backed troll who is digging a pit at the end of the rainbow, deep enough to bury a sullen pot of lead. Be sure to read me after my death if you care to know.

"I never think of her novel as written by an actual person."
"The actual people to me are Matthew and Marilla and Anne."

Maude and Anne

A woman who splits her childhood in half.
A novel knitting itself out of its own entrails.
A person being interviewed about her life.

in a photograph

What if your son decides to edit his mother's journals?
What if he takes out all of your least-noble thoughts?
Ever wonder what a slim volume your published journals might turn out to be?

in Boston
with L. C. Page.

Why do marriages lose their meaning? Why do husbands barely come home? Why do measles and broken lampshades take over one's life? Why do people tire of life? Why does the rainbow glow disappear in the grind of the day? Why does one fear to look in the mirror? Why do others judge us so harshly? Why does another person's opinion become one's own?

A writer whose skin is so thin as to offer no protection.

And you, Nora – you. Should I mention your children at all? But then I've already heard. We have never held anything back. You always kept your head above water. Nothing ever dragged you down. You are still a bird in flight.

Hardship never diminishes you. Remember all those poems we quoted? Two kindred spirits from the summer of 1903?

Chapter 13

Characters learn to judge an author. Here you succeed! – here you fail! Woe to the author who faces rebellion. Better episodes! – better descriptions! – better words! Who would want to read this novel? – who could read it if they should try? A better author would make a better work of art!

A novelist a little afraid to read a review.

Once more the doctor – the doctor once more. I don't know what's wrong with me, Doctor – I don't know what's wrong with you, Mrs. Montgomery. Do you think these pills are helping me, Doctor? – Do you think these pills are helping you, Mrs. Montgomery? There's another new pill on the market. Wouldn't hurt to give it a try. After all, what could be worse than what we seem to have now?

To be

A swimmer gradually drifting out to sea.
Two china dogs that guard a house.
An author who feels like a sorrel mare.

a little ship

What is your relationship with your husband, Ewan?
With Chester, your elder son?
With Stuart, your younger son?

sailing out of a safe harbour.

The pleasant consciousness of the still outdoors.
Light and flawless as the heart of a diamond.
Trails of saffron and rosy cloud.

Anne and Diana – Diana and Anne. Visiting all the old dear spots all over again. Lovers Lane – Haunted Wood – Crystal Lake. 'Do you remembers' again and again. Fifteen years old and kindred spirits. Not a worry – not a care.

The chapter writes itself – my pen has wings.
Writing the first page of the novel, Anne of Windy Poplars.

Returning to Anne. I owe a book to Anne. It will be *Anne of Windy Poplars*. Anne will be front and centre – no more waiting in the wings. Anne as she was – Anne as she is – in her early days. Anne as the principal of a school. Anne as a teacher – a friend – a guide. Anne bringing light into darkened corners. Anne as a candle – a lamp – a lighthouse. Anne as a beacon to people adrift on stormy seas.

Eventually, the little girl grew into a woman of some sixty years. Far beyond the age at which her young mother had died. And she could look back over the span of all those years. But she couldn't see her mother – her mother wasn't there. She was still the little girl who had no mother – simply because her mother had up and died.

"Once in a while, I get the feeling that she's worried about a number of things."
"She seems so certain that there's going to be another war."

Walking along with Di. Di is enraptured with my tale of how I poisoned myself. I am holding her spellbound with my dying agonies. The house is in need of painting. The porch is tumble-down. The garden is a jungle full of weeds. She'll see. She can't help but see. Oh, why did I invite her home with me?

Falling apart at the seams - a deliberate act of will - drawing back the camera - feel what he is thinking - the last chance he'll ever have - refuses to talk about it - spend his life in a bottle - might at first appear - the actor in full performance - withdraws to protect her.

Anne of Green Gables is the only world I know, Mrs. Montgomery. Anything outside this book is a world that I cannot see. Anything beyond the covers of this novel is unknown to me.

You remember the end of the novel? Oh how silly – of course you do. It was in your mind before it was known to me.

Well – I'm poised to begin my future. Remember the phrase, "all's right with the world"? How often I go and stand on that very last page.

The two agreed that they were
not prepared to live together
in the same home.
"Buy my half from me,"
said the one to the other,
"and I will go and live somewhere else."

"Buy my half from me,"
said the other to the one,
"and I will go and live somewhere else."

One could make a whole novel of one meeting of the CAA. Make a list while others chatter of dates and times. A novel of characters, mean and kind. Of some who sail and some who sink – of some who soar and some who crash. Of some who are beaten and some whose beatings are yet to come. Of some whose armour is thin as gossamer – of some whose fingers itch to wield the blood-stained club. Of some whose scars are only visible to those who can see. Who is living in a world of dreams? Who is dreaming of unreachable heights? Who is dreaming of coffee and sandwiches at the break? No – I don't believe I will write of the CAA.

A publisher for whom a book is a sacred vessel.
Chester Macdonald – Chester Macdonald. Oh from whence has come the seed? Cursed at birth, it would seem. But tell me – cursed by whom? Cursed by father? – cursed by mother? Cursed by Satan? – cursed by God? You are a scourge for all you encounter. Grasp the snake and it turns and stings you. Are you as miserable – in your quiet moments – as you have made me?

Oh this sounds like a cruel story. 'The cruel stepmother works her ill.' But sometimes life echoes fiction. Sometimes fairy-tales come true. Wicked stepmothers sometimes thrive in the everyday world.

Working on a new novel about Anne.
Calling it *Anne of Windy Poplars*.

It is the wedding of my beau. He is marrying someone else. I sit and listen as the wedding vows are said. Those whom God has joined together – do you take this girl as your wife. I mutter bitterly at every word I hear. I fidget with my finger. I remembered his beautiful speech as he pled his troth. I wonder if he will ask me to give her my ring.

Rises again and again - filled with infinite promise - not another living creature - a strange road - you were so hopeful - another has taken her place - the essence of hell itself - who commands my pen - almost ready to fly - struggle through snowdrifts.

Yes, I am dying to know my future. Perhaps it will be glorious and grand. I can't believe it will be anything short of enchanted.
Why are we born if not for adventure? Imagination draws us on to other worlds. Why should we leave even one of these worlds unexplored?
Oh, I do hope you've made up your mind. Oh, I hope you will set me free. Oh, Mrs. Montgomery, what is the life that is waiting for me?

*A glance
from time to time
as people
buy the fish.*

Anne as a mother – Anne as a wife. I see a woman with a mystery illness. Doctor to doctor – who is right? What the illness? – what the cure? Will she recover? – will she die? Let me think a while and the rest will come to me.
A reviewer who always knows what he likes.
Windy Poplars strains at its tether. The novel is trying to run away. Anne is surrounded by darkness and death. Is everyone miserable in this world? Why does everything in life turn out so wrong? A bitter, bitter person – a bitter person who is at Anne's elbow every minute of every day. Don't tell me that life is kind – don't tell me that life is gentle – life is a sea and I am drowning in its waves. A young and lonely person – her mother died and her father left town – a person continually searching for her own name. Anne is perplexed as to how to help her. Life is quicksand and I am slowly sinking down.

A driver who keeps running into the ditch.
An interviewer who asks a very good question.
A man who wears a bandana around his head.

*"And I will seal
these lips of mine.
I shall not
talk of dread.*

How do you get along with your parishioners?
With the members of the authors' group?
How about your family and friends back in P.E.I.?

Sitting in the ditch. What are we to do? It will be hours before daylight comes. A car with four boys comes along and they lift us out. Do they notice my husband inside, clutching the wheel?

*Fell down, got up,
Fell down again.
I could not see my way.*

Old age came, as it does to everyone.

Lack of any other name - all I know about it - imagine things - dreams don't often come true - gave him the naming of her - call me cordelia - they didn't want her - he was a kindred spirit - what I imagine about myself - how old are you.

Pantries crammed to overflowing.
The wind blowing cheerfully through the silver-grey maple wood.
Three lean hump-backed old spruce trees.

Seemed so big to them - going to run away - a perception of the loveliness of the world - she wasn't anybody - stabbed completely through - she was sick-and-tired - tyrannize over you - walk through the graveyard - not the girl I thought you were - no story for children.

Always strange to read about oneself in the newspapers. Well, not of oneself, exactly – but of Anne. A new *Anne of Green Gables* movie is in the works. Not a cent for me, of course. An actor has flown, overnight, from New York to Hollywood and appeared before the cameras the very next day. He is playing the character, Matthew – Matthew whose sorrel mare and buggy jogged along at a different pace so long ago – on his way to meet Anne – Anne who sat on the shingles and wondered what lay ahead. Matthew and Anne and me – not one of the three of us had any idea where the old sorrel mare would lead. And now Matthew takes an airplane from New York to Hollywood. Presumably, Anne – the actress, Anne – is already there. Perhaps they'll meet by a swimming pool – sipping daiquiris as they talk. Anne could effuse over palm trees and oranges – Matthew could drive a Cadillac – a White Mansion of Delight in the distance with gables of green.

A character who would like to sue the author.

Oh Frede – Frede – Frede. I had such fear that you would die. You were my Diana – and you are gone. But one cannot speak to the dead – I know – I have tried. And what about the books? – does this mean that I should have Diana die?

At least she didn't expect him to talk. And she didn't ask him any questions after the one about the red of the roads. She told him all about the journey. She opened up his eyes. She made him see a shining lake instead of a pond.

"She must have felt quite strongly about the Great War."
"That's the only time she didn't play the supporting wife."

One of those twins from up at Ingleside. No she doesn't look like her mom. "I just think it isn't fair", the child is saying. "She should be the fairy queen in the Sunday School play. Cassie Thomas should be me and I should be her." So Dovie Johnson has told her a tale. The world is an oyster whose pearls are all lies. I remember the two different nights they were both of them born. Now what, I wonder, should I choose to tell this child?

A stinking skeleton - wherever za would go - share each other's thoughts - it doesn't bother me - my great life-change - the problem is in believing - living in the shadows - some little gem - sometimes i catch myself - every word i leave behind.

Ann of Green Gables hasn't been sunshine every day. There's the trouble with Marilla's eyes. Near the end of the novel, I visit Matthew's grave.

I've seen storm clouds over the ocean. Clutched at my coat in the driving rain. Hurried to school while glancing up at an ominous sky.

So I accept the fact that life will come and get me. No matter where I am or what I am doing. It will do its best or it will do its worst.

I am ready for 'all and sundry'. That's a phrase that I read in a book. 'All and sundry' means that I want to have a full life.

Some of his mates had been swept to sea.
Other mates had braved the waves.
The boy was just above the waves that lashed the mast.

Grinding away at the novel. Writing with blood and bone and marrow, though no one will ever know. As light as air – a child-like bubble in the passing breeze. A year of planning – on and off. A freight-train rush and a four-month first draft. Now for a month or two of polish to a final draft. The end of life for Anne. I don't believe in tearful farewells. A couple of donkeys hitched to a cart. Shrug your backpack on, my Anne, and set off on your own.

A reader who is disappointed in a book.

Taking control of *Windy Poplars*. A darkened core – a cheerful frame. The outer-frame is Anne and Gilbert – the coming-together of girl and boy. Boy and girl together – boy and girl apart – boy and girl together at the end. Anne is a solver of others' problems. Others are cradled in her arms. Gilbert finishes medical school – Anne resigns her principal's post. They return to the world of Green Gables and Avonlea. Every book should end with a wedding and a feast.

What did Mrs. Spencer know that she didn't mention? What did the little girl know that she wasn't going to tell? If we keep her she'll have a decent home and proper schooling. If we send her back it will be to who knows what. What would be practical about sending the little girl back?

Windy Poplars is nearing its end.
This is me and my Anne on a farewell tour.

We glide beneath a canopy of white. Apple trees in snowy fragrant bloom. I lose my sense of speech. I do not move nor do I speak. I ignore the dogs that bark and the noisy boys. I don't speak for at least three miles. I ask about the name, once again. Matthew tells me – once again – that he calls it the Avenue. I name it – once again – the White Way of Delight. Matthew is smiling as I am talking. His mind is gradually acquiring more scope. His imagination is gradually feeling a gentle breeze. I can feel what he is thinking. Kindred spirits he and I. I feel that I can tell him everything.

Insists that we are lost - what could be worse - the things you know - write an ending - too early for me to tell - fires on the beach - turn it all into words - a shelf too high to reach - a very happy year - watching a rainbow dance.

Please Mrs. Montgomery. You never tell me about your life. But I'm sure that you've seen sunshine and you've seen rain.

Please Mrs. Montgomery – please. You have had a full life, I am sure. What you have enjoyed would you deny to me?

How soon am I to know? How soon are you going to decide? How soon am I to know what my future life will be?

But wait! – oh I beg you, Mrs. Montgomery!

Do not withhold my future life from me! I implore you to give me a chance! Let me grow up and take the sunshine and the rain!

I'll take the darkness in my stride! Make me as human as I can be! Even death in childbirth is preferable – don't you see!

What you propose would be death as well – death in a childhood that has no future! You would be keeping a corpse alive – the corpse of the child I used to be!

Oh Mrs. Montgomery! – I am begging you to listen! *Anne of Green Gables* can only live if I am a true and complete human being to future readers! It will die if it is a fiction and I am a sham!

Dreams chase us
and we chase our dreams.

William Arthur Deacon. The man behind the veil. The wizard behind the curtain of the CAA. It was not entirely by surprise. There was a noticeable lack of eye-contact on the night of the vote. Small groups were whispering in corners – people barely returning 'hello'. The vote was crushing; I kept my composure. I am no longer on the executive of the CAA.

A book which is as indifferent as a cat.

I have come so near the surface. All they can see – if they look – are my eyes. The alligator who lies in wait while watching its prey. The alligator is never sleeping, though he might wait for a hundred years. Oh, your slim new volume of poems! Congratulations on your monumental feat! I've written ten volumes on the contents of the alligator's craw. My words are as sharp as primeval teeth. My tail shall lash your petty poems from the shelf.

"Reverend Macdonald was very active in the recruiting of volunteers."
"Never once did she appear by his side."

The girl created a world

Readers who look through a character's eyes.
A novel which seems to write itself.
A person with a dreadful feeling that things will go wrong.

in which her other girl

Have you sketched out scenes and chapters?
Have a few notebooks hidden away?
Would such a novel be your lasting masterpiece?

could live.

Bye this boke! – oh, bye this boke! There are those who need the jobs! – there are those who need the work! Pity the men who make the paper! – pity the men who make the ink! Pity their children and their wives! Bye this boke! – oh bye this boke! Lives can be changed for a penny or two! Oh please, Mister, won't you buy this book!
Writing the last page of the novel, Anne of Windy Poplars.
Cuts! – I am asked to make cuts! I am asked to make cuts to *Windy Poplars*! Something about the balance – how I have balanced the light and the dark. Fear that the darkness just might damage the movie sale. Oh I long to leave Anne behind. Anne is not a one for these times – no more than am I. I take a vow – I take a pledge – I shall put my Anne on the shelf. I shall never write an Anne-novel – ever again.

Chapter 14

So here we are, all you readers – Anne will soon be landing at the dock. *Anne of Ingleside* will be the best that I can do. But don't bother to read it carefully – just bounce along on the surface – just skim along on the top and leave the rest. Take no thought of the caverns-of-self that lie underground. Hold Anne back if she notices a cave and wants to explore. Soon she will have another book – a tranquil island in a hostile sea – another book for her to roam around inside. But I promise you that there is more to come – a whole lot more. My son has promised to be faithful. Not a kindred spirit at all, but a boy who made a promise to his mom. Someday, he'll print the other words I write.

A novel being cradled in a reader's hands.

Oh these drugs. I hate these drugs. The doctors force them down my throat. They make me weep – they make me dream – poked and singed by the flames of hell. I cannot think – I cannot read – I cannot write.

To ignore

Characters who jostle at the feed-bowl.
A young woman with skin as tough as an alligator.
A maid counting the spoons when the guests have gone.

the drifting snow

What are the agonies that a person like you has suffered?
What are the crushing defeats that you have undergone?
What are the dreams that, in your life, have come crashing down?

and the biting wind.

Living in a world where there are Octobers.
A huge bowl of crimson and sapphire.
Maple boughs in an old blue jug on a table.

But what of Shirley – forgotten Shirley? What of Shirley, as the novel draws to a close? I have put everyone in the spotlight except little Shirley. I sit at my desk by the window and gently massage my brain. I need a story for Shirley. Some little gem for Shirley. If I sit here something will occur before too long.

A writer who swears she will never write again.

The correspondence piles up on my desk. 'L. M. Montgomery' to you, if you read my books. 'Maud' to you, if you knew me in P.E.I. 'Anne' to you, perhaps, if you live in Avonlea. I choose my names quite carefully when I am contemplating my books. Ever wonder if I have chosen a name for you?

So what became of the little girl? What became of the little girl? What did the little girl come to be? She grew up like everyone else. She married and had children – like everyone else.

"A good book is a personal friend."
"Anne has been my personal friend since I read her book."

It is a warm sunny day! I am in the Cavendish cemetery! A funeral is taking place! Many mourners have gathered around an open grave! There is a casket setting on trestles! The casket is open with a corpse inside! I move among the mourners! Some look up and some do not! I look down at the casket! The corpse is me!

Cursed with imagination - able to function - which roads to take - balanced the light and the dark - she shines a lantern - pouring poison into her dream - driving and muttering and shouting - creeping in the darkness - never be able to plan - she was the cause.

Ours is a very strange relationship, Anne. Not a normal one, I know. There is a very unique rapport between we two.

I am the author. You are the character. And *I* am the one who created *you*.

An orphan – Anne – is a person without her feet on the ground. I realize that you are grateful to Matthew and Marilla. But – in a very real sense – *I* am the one who adopted you.

"But I have no money to buy
your half of the house,"
said the one.
"Nor do I have money to buy
your half of the house,"
said the other.

1919 was the most excruciatingly agonizing year that I have endured while I have been alive on this earth. And this is not counting all the grief that

Chester has caused. Troubles breed and multiply. While I was struggling with the plague of Ewan, then was visited upon my person the Chester curse.

A publisher who loves to sit and read a good book.

Meeting Nora after all these years. Oh Nora – lovely Nora. Twenty-four, to be exact. The young and gifted two of 1903. So how have you been? – but don't even answer – I can see it in your face. Life has been kind-enough to leave you as you are. My books? – oh yes, my books. How kind of you to say. Many people I meet don't mention them at all.

The girl went home – she missed the island. Time passed – her father grew ill. He wrote her letters while he could – by the bushelful. Finally the stepmother wrote that he was too ill to write. And that was the only letter the stepmother wrote.

Writing *Anne of Ingleside.*
Trying to think of a story for Shirley.

The minister begins the service! "We shall now speak well of the dead!" Every mourner opens a book and begins to read! All of the mourners read at once! Dozens of voices rise and fall! The sun is shining down on the casket! The voices drone in murmured contentment! The honeyed tongues of satisfied bees! Every mourner is reading from a novel which was written by me!

No gift for anne - prove you wrong - something that they are not - control over me - something of me - getting ready for an occasion - two cycles will interact - a cage with metal bars - i am exhausted - the beasts are snarling.

But the thing is, Anne – the unpleasant reality happens to be – that a real orphan grows up. And you are not a real orphan, Anne. You are orphan in a book.

And I – oh, I do hope you'll forgive me – want to protect you from growing up in the world that I have come to know. You recall that I had Marilla think that very thing. You weren't there, of course, as she was thinking, but now you know.

Until you told me, I didn't realize that this would be so. I didn't realize that every word of the novel would be known to you. You have more scope for the imagination than I had thought.

A glance,
here and there,
as people
buy the produce of the farm.

Shirley doesn't have a story. I sit by the window and watch the birds. The clock reminds me that the morning is moving along. My mind is blank – my mind is numb. I have nothing to offer Shirley. My well is as dry as dry. If I sit here for hours, I know that nothing will come.

A reviewer who reads too many books.

My veins are filled with ink. I have no blood at all. I pricked myself with a pen and drained every last drop. My heart pumps more easily now, though the early scars still show. Early on, I lived my life – now I write my life instead. As long as the memory of pain is alive, the ink will flow.

A stranger who is asked to write an 'obitchery'.
A dead baby who lies in a cold cold grave.
A twin who dwells inside her other half.

"Suffice to say,
Suffice to say,
that all
will not be well.

What is the greatest height which you have ever attained?
What is the lowest depth to which you have descended?
Was there a moment at which you said 'I cannot go on'?

Sitting in the car. Surrounded by walls of fog. We have no idea where we are. Ewan rants and raves and foams. He insists that he knows how to drive a car.

Slashed by bramble.
Cut by thorn.
Felt blood upon my hands.

Not eager to leave, but willing, just the same.

Might be called friendship - set fire to the house - the brand you wanted - before she could confess - can't be perfectly happy - afraid going over bridges - an unromantic name - beauty-loving eyes - those trees and flowers - a thistle or a skunk cabbage - I do wish she'd lived.

Winds crouching when they come to the rocks.
Tinted leaves drifting slowly down.
Glowing fires, comfort, shelter from storms.

Hold all the threads - imprisoned like a canary - just a lot of old trees and cows - clung to her identity frantically - her own inner life - her heart had been wholly buried - wouldn't let anyone use me - the shadow had withdrawn - the mask paralysed her with terror - what daffodils were thinking about.

Four months on *Anne of Ingleside*. From September to December without a break. I put everything out of my mind and plunged ahead. Briars and brambles – thistles and thorns. With a few mums and marigolds in the mix. This is me – and this is not me – no one but me could ever know. The little assault is the big assault – the big offence is the little offence. What I want to write and what I feel I have to – what is for me and what is for all those readers out there. Some will see charm and some will see treacle, but only the children and I will be able to read what is truly, actually there. Not Susan Baker – not Gilbert and Anne. Just the children in the book – Jem and Walter and Nan and Di and Shirley and – yes, and little Rilla, too – know what gems I have sewn in the lining of *Ingleside*. What I gain and what I give up – what I will never get back again. Every drop of ink was distilled from a drop of blood.

A character who splits the seams of a book.

Not every day should be sunny. There's always the porch during summer downpours. The grass grows greener when the ditches are swollen with rain. The cistern under the down-spout fills to the brim. We know the sun will come again. This we know – this we know. The problem is in believing that which we know.

And the White Way of Delight. He'd never noticed it before. Well, not the way she saw it. Not with a pair of open eyes. He always thought that apple-blossoms meant apples soon.

"When I read one of her books, I feel transported into an entirely different world."

"I would love to go and live in P.E.I."

I stand and shout for attention! I demand the right to read! All the mourners stop reading and stare! I clutch a handful of sheets of paper! "I bring the truth among you! I insist that you listen to me!" The wind blows cold and the sky grows dark! A gale is blowing up at sea! I clutch the papers tight in my fingers! I read the words from the fluttering pages I hold in my hand! I shout to try to make the mourners hear!

On the right road - to judge an author - success rolls off - a doctor to please yourself - confined on a shelf - strife and problems enough - the story isn't really true - an entirely different world - breaking it apart - in a position to rescue.

But I still have power over you, Anne. A power that Marilla doesn't have. And I will use that power with kindness and forethought, I promise you.

Yes, I realize that my decision will affect you. It will affect what happens to you for the rest of your life. And it will affect what you are able to do in response to what happens to you for the rest of your life.

Matthew is gone – I realize, of course, that I can't go back on that. But Marilla and Diana are there, and so are you and Gilbert Blythe. And to put it bluntly, Anne – I can move you all like chessmen on a board.

The wind was shrieking in the rigging.
Waves were pounding at the wreck.
He was shouting but we couldn't hear his voice.

Perhaps Anne has too many children. Oh what a terrible thought to have. No, I must think of something for Shirley. What is a birthday without a present? A holiday without a treat? There must be a story – there must be a story. It is on a shelf in my mind. A Christmas present in August, wondering when the big day will come. A Christmas present on a shelf too high to reach.

A reader who frowns and throws away a book.

Chester driving me to meetings. Chester driving me to shop. His cold and icy silence. I well know the game that he is playing. Leaving me out to freeze in the dark. A faithful dog chained and whimpering in his master's yard.

So – let's see now – what was there on the farm that a girl could do? The girl was bright enough to learn. The girl could be taught to cook and sew. Help with the weeding in the garden. Go to the coop, every morning, and collect the eggs.

Trying to find a story for Shirley.
I sit for hours but my mind is still a blank.

"Mrs. Montgomery has to be about the most normal person one could ever expect to meet. Amazing when you think that she's a best-selling author, with a string of books that are being read around the world. The creator of the immortal Anne of P.E.I. I just happened to be sitting next to her at one of these functions. There was a delay in serving the main course – a problem in the kitchen, I believe. 'Do you have a family, Mrs. Montgomery?' I tentatively asked. 'Oh yes. I have a husband and two boys.' That was all I asked, but she offered more information, as easy as you please. 'My husband was a minister – retired now, for a number of years. My oldest son is studying law. My youngest son is studying medicine. I don't live far from here – close enough to Toronto to remain within the orbit of the literary scene. I like to write – and to garden – I divide my time between the two. A quiet life is best for the writing – don't you agree?' She kept folding the edge of the tablecloth as she talked. Folding and unfolding and folding it again."

Every blister, cyst and boil - the snake-oil salesmen - they take them away - goodbye to the asylum - only a baddums-dream - give up all control - as bright as bright - what becomes of a plan - i fought so hard - they become dangerous.

Anne – I did not speak with you in order to ask for your advice. I merely meant to reminisce for a few moments and to give you the news about the forthcoming series of books. That you have given me so much to think about has come to me as quite a surprise.

We are all born into a world in which decisions have already been made – decisions which have a series of effects on our future lives. Is it with kindness that I remind you that you are a character. It is with firmness that I remind you that I am an author.

I insist that I make this decision on my own. Perhaps here – at this thought– is where you and I must part ways. You will find out my decision when you find yourself living your future life – between the covers of our next Anne-book.

Some dreams stay.
Some dreams leave.
Some refuse to leave.

Looking out onto Lake Ontario. The trees are bare and the lake is grey. Many things have not been right for days and days. But I can see springtime on the island. I don't even have to close my eyes. Raindrops lying on nasturtium leaves beside the brook. Dragonflies glittering over the water. Daisies nodding to me with white and gold laughter. I could go on and on, but a moment or two will suffice. There have been terrifying days when this power has failed me. I can take anything at all – earthquakes, tornadoes, raging fires – as long as I can create a world of my own. A moment out of time is all I need.

A book which singes the hands and sears the soul.

Two people sitting on a bench. Anne and I – side by side. Gradually one of the two begins to fade – the other begins to grow in size. The sun shines – the birds sing. All is well in the land of the ill. One person sitting alone on a bench.

"I can't figure out why she left the island if she loves it so much."
"The wife has to follow the husband – that's how it works."

Anne and Maude
and Mary Miles Minter

A talkative girl who is speechless for at least three miles.
A boy who makes a promise to his mom.
An author with an idea for a story.

in a photograph

What do you owe to the reading public?

What do you owe to your books?
What do you owe to the characters that you create?

in front of
the Hollywood sign.

Why do some people not have a story? Why are some people lost in the crowd? Doesn't everyone feel a sense of importance inside? Why are some people not noticed? Invisible to the naked eye? Only a person to themselves and to no one else? Am I a story-teller or a secret-keeper? My readers are sitting and waiting for stories around the fire. Why, then, do I have no story that I can tell?
An author who struggles to reach the very last page.
Suffer the little children. The little children of this parish. How I envy their kindness, their generosity, their willingness to learn. Their smiles, their angel voices, their delight at simple things. Why do children have to grow up to be adults?

Chapter 15

My mother died when I was less than two. My father left me to go and live in the West. Name me one orphan who felt that she was loved? The world has given me fame. They believe that I am Anne – they believe that the two of us live in Avonlea.

A person living in past and present simultaneously.

Oh that's a very good question. Now let me see – let me see. What is my life at this moment in time? Well, I am currently working on a new novel. It is set in my old haunts in P.E.I. Yes, Anne is what you might call 'the protagonist'. She is what is called 'my bread and butter' in the trade. Though I think there's a time-limit on everything – don't you agree? Whether on butter or on bread – or on milk? There is a time when they become dangerous to eat or to drink.

To look

A novel which is planned as having two cycles.
A boy whose uncle tells him he can't have a dog.
A man who has no practical thoughts in his head.

like the Anne

Suppose you take everything that you have ever written?
That which is published and that which is not?
Every thought you've ever turned into ink on a page?

of Green Gables days.

A light shining through a gap in the trees.
The wild cherry trees along the lane.
A sky pale, golden and ethereal.

Oh you generation of vipers. Free to speak while I could not. Every parasite – every gossip – every assassin of character. All the venom of a rabid quilting bee. I spent all those years in agony. I was crucified in the dark. The target of every axe and spear. Covered with honey – covered with ants. I spent those years being tortured while tied to a tree.

A person for whom the past is never past.

What is the state of my life at this time? I was a minister's wife, of course. I was such for many, many years. At Leaskdale and at Zephyr and then at Norval as well. We are retired now, my husband and I. We no longer have the burden of a charge. Of course, we shall always have our pleasant memories. And we do go back and visit from time to time.

So that is the story of the little girl. That is the story of the little girl. The little girl who had no mother. The little girl who had no mother from the age of less than two. The little girl whose mother up and died.

"They seem like a very devoted couple."
"She's always helping him when he can't seem to find the words."

They don't want me to have my dog. My uncle told me so. He said my aunt don't want me to have a dog. She liked it when it was a puppy. Now she don't want me to have it. Why do people go back on their word? They put it in the paper. Someone is coming to have a look. People give you things and then they take them away.

Cannot be just an illusion - keep turning to ice - my world of the pen - too small for his dreams - what's in my head - totally and completely wrong - so blissfully unaware - deep in my mind - wings are heavily-laden - the dream is all too true.

I have always thought that I would love to be a writer. I think that a writer must be a most wonderful thing to be. A writer like I imagine you – Mrs. Montgomery – to be.

I would be able to live two lives. Or many lives, as far as that goes. I could imagine any life that occurred to me.

Of course, I live inside a book. So I have no control, you see. I have no control over anything at all.

"Yes I can cut it down the middle,"
said the carpenter,
"and make two separate houses
out of what was once one home.
There will be a gap the width of a saw-blade
between the two halves.
Now – shall I send the bill to one address
or two?"

Oh Ewan. I feel revulsion – at even the thought of your touch. You were young and handsome and carried yourself so well. But look at what you have become. An empty hulk – a rotting shell – a stinking skeleton on the beach. You are tormented – crazed – alone. Oh I am afraid that what has happened to you is gradually – very gradually – happening to me. Except that I can walk and talk, as you cannot. My worst nightmare is that I am slowly becoming you.

One for whom characters are people and people are characters.

As to my health – I simply take it day to day. I am not as young as I was – nor is anyone else. Perhaps it's the curse of the writer – you simply get used to sleepless nights. I am still capable of working for very long hours. I write and I garden – I try to balance out my day. Sometimes I just sit at the window with a cup of tea. Yes, I let my mind drift back to P.E.I.

What did her father think about as his very life was ebbing? About the fact that his wife gave birth to a little girl. How his bosom swelled as he stood on the porch in the moonlight. How his wife and new young daughter were the finest things in his life. Tears rolled down his cheeks as he thought of them.

Nearing the end of *Anne of Ingleside*.
We are riding in the buggy, Anne and I.

Jem Blythe is lost. Jem Blythe is sleeping soundly. He has had a busy day and is lost to the world. Mother and Susan are searching the house. The men have started searching the town. There is talk of dragging the pond. But little Jem is not lost. I am asleep on the window seat. Will anyone think to look behind the door where I like to go when I want to be lost and found?

Our pleasant memories - the finest things in life - follow your daydreams - nothing ever need be said - any challenge or any concern - what is truly, actually there - if all went well - if i were sitting on a shelf - will turn against you - live her life again.

Of course, I wouldn't expect to control the events of my *own* life. I realize that wouldn't be entirely fair. Not even *writers* control the lives they are living, day by day.

On that, I am willing to take my chances. Just as I did when I was an orphan and looking for a home. I accept the idea that *you* have created *me*.

But I would also be a writer, just like you, Mrs. Montgomery. I would create a world with my pen and my imagination. I would create the life of a character, in my turn.

Will they ever grow up?
Always glance and shy away?

Are the clocks at the market all on hold?

I despise my own son. Yes, Chester, I do. The upside-down and inside-out of everything I hoped you would be. I carried you inside me. You lurk inside me still. You are the curse that I have loosed upon the world. Where is your wife? Where are your children? Where do you slither in the depths of the night? Woe to me that I have been a mother to you.
One whose birth takes place inside a book.
Oh, I have readers all over the world. Readers in Denmark and Japan. I have been translated into Dutch and German and French. I get letters almost every day in the mail. Anne is a little girl to these people – as alive as are you and me. They ride along with her in the buggy – look through her eyes at the White Way of Delight. They all hope to be adopted. Yes – they all feel like orphans, in some strange way.

A fly which is drowning in ink.
A person who sprinkles others with hopes and dreams.
A father who writes stacks and stacks of letters.

"*What I have seen,*
What I have heard,
is not for me to say.

All of the novels about Anne Shirley?
All of the novels about other characters?
All of your poems and all of your journals?

Daylight comes and we can see. He starts the car and we proceed. We are on the right road for home but Ewan insists that we are lost. He gets out on the road and mutters to himself. I hold the fragments of Ewan together with my bare hands.

Could feel the glow,
Could smell the glow
but never saw the ring.

She retained just one fervent wish as her candle burned so low.

Might have been considered indicative - groaned in spirit - have a white dress - black as the raven's wing - so many things to like - no need to be ashamed - so many lovely places - the orchard and the brook - I've never seen that house - that left me an orphan.

Green wreaths tied with huge bows of red ribbon.

Carpets of rich green mosses along the banks.
Bees buzzing in the white clover.

Lovely red-gold hair - wanted to study them - painted her dying agonies - would be of no account to them - realms of wonder and romance - the secret of immortal youth - call her soul her own - those pearls aren't real pearls - the stars were laughing at her - i'm jutht tired of being me.

I practice my smile as the children line up at the zoo. When are you going to write a better book than *Anne of Green Gables*? An Anne without any problems? – an Anne without any strife? I have strife and problems enough in my daily world. When will you write another young-Anne? Why does Anne have to grow old? We liked it better when you and Anne were in Avonlea.
One who shapes her life as if writing a book.
Yes, I attend the meetings of the authors' association. It makes for a pleasant evening of literary chat. Of course, we don't all write the same kinds of novels. Some are very different from the kind that pay my bills. But how can writers be compared? I never talk of readers or sales. I never mention that I have readers around the world. That I get letters from people who say I have changed their lives. Readers who say that I transport them to P.E.I.

And then she picked out the farm at Green Gables. Closed her eyes and had a dream. Then she opened her eyes and pointed it out to him. She had imagined ever detail with her eyes closed. He couldn't do that and he had lived there all his life.

"The minister is always the public face of the couple."
"It's the minister's wife who often pulls the strings."

The Ladies Aid quilting bee at Ingleside. Ladies come from miles around. Busy fingers keep the time for idle tongues. Quilts for mothers with brand-new babies. Quilts for children cuddling and cold. Quilts for aging or pneumatics, waiting to die. All in an afternoon's good work. Dedicated to the glory of God. Whether heeded or not, some truths are being told.

Truly call my home - waving to anne - the time that was intolerable - alone at the circus - counting all the grief - the grunting hunch-backed troll - letting the rainy days go - cannot she see - tired of being herself - i am slowly becoming you.

I wonder – do you write your books by hand or on a typewriter? Do you take a notebook everywhere you go? Do you wake up in the middle of the night and jot down your ideas?
I could write books and send them out to grateful readers. I could get mail

from all over the world as you say you do. It would be wonderful to be the person who brings such joy.

So I'm wondering just where you get your ideas. Do you have a routine that you follow every day? I'm sure that you must be leading a wonderful life.

There were fires on the beach.
Darkness hid him from our sight.
In the morning he'd be there or he'd be gone.

Utter terror at the world! Utter revulsion at what it is and what I am! Two world wars!– two world wars! Millions of dead and another one on the way! I am a disciple of King Lear. If the world is not perfect – I do not want to live in it. If I am not perfect – I do not want to live in the world. I wrote a novel in which I tried to escape from both. We are all in a house – in the middle of the night – and the black water is rising through the floorboards. What does it matter whether any of us know how to swim?

One who spends her entire life inside a book.

Oh, the park in P.E.I. – yes, of course. It's called 'the Green Gables Park'. On land that the government set aside. Of course there was never an actual house – not an actual 'Green Gables' house. I put several houses together in the book. People forget that Anne is fiction – though all the places are real. You can drink from the Dryad's Bubble – just like Anne. No, I don't go back too often – I'm in the Toronto orbit now. They don't make me pay for a ticket when I do.

But we're not going to call her Cordelia – not such an impractical name as that. Never heard such a name before. Never heard anyone on the island called by that name. If she stays, she'll have to go by her real name. Nobody in this house is going to pretend they're somebody else.

Nearing the end of *Anne of Ingleside.*
Just ahead, I can see the White Way of Delight.

We are on the crest of a hill. We look down on Barry's pond. I name it the Lake of Shining Waters once again. We go over the bridge again and around the corner. The sun has set, but I can see everything as clear as clear. The dark church spire. The little valley. The gentle slope with farms all along. And on the left, back from the road, the woods and the blossoming trees. A star is shining in the sky overhead. We drive over Lynde's Hollow and we are home – Matthew and I. Marilla will be won over. Her imagination will acquire more scope. I am at home, at Green Gables, once again.

The plan is firm and final - sounds like a cruel story - insists that we are fine - searching the darkness - not going to blink - lingering in the neighbour-

hood - all the dear old spots - as close as any two souls - invisible to the naked eye - as if you are in the room.

Do you base your stories on the things that have happened to you? You said you lost your parents early – that you, yourself, were an orphan of sorts. It that the source of the life that you gave to me?

Perhaps my character's life could be based on yours, Mrs. Montgomery. Did you not say you have a husband and some strapping sons? It would be fun to model my character's life on you.

Perhaps if you told me more about your life, Mrs. Montgomery. It sounds like a wonderful life to me. Perhaps my character could be a writer just like you.

One can spend an eon
trying to shed a dream.

And my Anne – oh my Anne. Oh, I hope that you are not me. But you have followed me around – to Leaskdale – to Norval – to Swansea. I see you lingering in the neighbourhood when I go out for a walk. You have knocked on my door and asked to live in my house. Oh Anne – oh precious Anne. I hope you are not me, as I am not you.

A pile of words on a desk awaiting form.
Of course you can ask about my family.

My husband is now retired. We were partners for many years. Both of us hitched up to the church as to a plough. Oh no – my writing is strictly my own – I have no partner there. He has the respect of his former parishioners. He preaches on special occasions now. Yes, his health is of some concern, but is under control. A quiet life is what's best for my husband now.

Yes my oldest son is named 'Chester'. At present, Chester is studying law. He has a wife and children. No, he has no plans to write. Though he has done some acting – in amateur presentations at church. In that he resembles me – in his interest in the arts. There are traits in which he resembles my husband as well.

Stuart is the youngest and second son. He has no attachments as yet. He is too young to think of marriage. He is attending university. Medicine seems to be his forté. Stuart is quite devoted to athletics. He's very successful at what he does. One more young person starting out on the road of life.

"Well she was the perfect minister's wife as far as I'm concerned."
"Supported him in his calling for all those years."

Maude and Anne

An Achilles without an Achilles Heel.

A character who offers to help an author cope.
A person who never shares her private thoughts.

in a photograph

And think of all you have written as one big, massive, many-thousand-word tome?
Would all of this, then, be the story of your life?
Or would there be something – something very important – still yet to write?

with Ewan
and Chester and Stuart.

It is all in my journals. I have recorded my darkest thoughts for fifty years. I have asked my son, Stuart, to publish them – every thought and every word. Thoughts about Ewan, thoughts about Chester, thoughts about relatives, neighbours, friends. Thoughts about fame and writing books – and, yes, thoughts about Anne. I made Stuart promise me – hand on heart and eye to eye. Not a word must you soften – not a word must you omit. Publish these journals when I am dead. I want everyone to know just who I am.
A book whose walls are developing cracks at the seams.
Well, I live a life of routine. I work quite hard at what I do. I'm hoping to finish *Anne of Ingleside* soon. When I complete it, I'll take a break. Library, movies, reading books – ones I haven't written, that is. Tending the garden in the summer – in the winter, hot toddy and a warm cosy fire. I'm starting to realize that I'm getting a little older. Yes, I am starting to feel my age. I don't travel as much as I used to. I have no plans to go back to the island anytime soon.

Chapter 16

Anne of Ingleside is complete – complete in manuscript, at last. Forty-one chapters of Anne and Gilbert and their brood. Nothing but Anne and her concerns for four whole months. Appropriate, I suppose, that I finish it in December – though, of course, it won't be published until next spring.

To be

A young girl and an older person on a buggy.
A person who feels trapped inside a dream.
A character on the brink of her future life.

a person who emits

You have been a novelist?
You have been a poet?
You have been a diarist as well?

an inner glow.

The mirth of wood-elves coming from every corner.
Gleaming white spaces and dark glens of spruce.
A girl wishing that a wild rose could talk.

Yes, *Anne of Ingleside* is done. For that, I feel such relief. At times I would look out the window, when the novel was not going well, and the word 'potboiler' would come to mind. Almost as if a grinch had written that word in the snow. And then I would take a break for a while – rub my eyes and ask the maid for a cup of tea. Perhaps do some correspondence or darn a sock. Then I'd apologize to Anne and get back to work.

So the little girl kept telling herself that she was not unique. She kept telling herself that other people had learned to live with what she thought of as a terrible thing. Had learned to put childish things away and become an adult. Had learned to let scars simply be scars. What is a scar if a warrior's arm can still heft the sword?

"Great artists are always tormented."
"That's how great art is made."

A human invented a puppet.
She made the puppet walk and talk
as humans do.

My best ideas - two people to manage - there was a clause - a cataclysm for me - a personal friend - life doesn't get better - never had no poetry - read and think again - her utmost dreams - wishes i wasn't alive.

So farewell, Anne. It has been so pleasant to talk. I always feel so welcome in Avonlea.

Two kindred spirits
got together in their dreams.
Maude and Anne – Anne and Maude.
Lover's Lane – Haunted Woods.
Each felt the need
of a do-you-remember day.

Every time a book of mine comes out, people read it and wonder who is who. Who is Jim Mowbray and who is Phillipa Abbey? – who is the uncle who lied to the boy about his dog? Some people might think that Susan Baker is me! Why not the old aunt who does nothing but complain? How naive of people to think that fiction is real. Of course, there are different kinds of real. Not one character in the book is a person whom I know – no, nor knew when we were all young and hopeful in Cavendish. But every one of these characters – every soul in *Anne of Ingleside* – has a presence that makes each one of them real to me.

The girl would often dream about her father. She always had such pleasant, cheerful dreams. Her father was always a man of infinite promise. His star would always shine as bright as bright. He would press her cheek to his in every dream.

Reaching the end of *Anne of Ingleside*.
Waving to Matthew and Marilla on the porch.

The human felt like a puppet.

*She felt she couldn't walk and talk
as humans do.*

To be lost and found - a person holding the fragments - a girl who wonders - imagine all kinds of things - a long-lost home - to take my chances - eyes are giving her trouble - a very strange relationship - if i were just me - questions that burn and singe.

I worry about you, Mrs. Montgomery. You have not kept your secrets very well. And you seem to have a need to tell me more.

Yes, you did – you did tell me about your family. When you were starting out on life. When you were optimistic and hoped that things would go well.

You once called us kindred spirits. While you were writing the book. You said that Diana would be that person for me.

*Two kindred spirits
took a tour of former scenes.
Anne and Maude – Maude and Anne.
Idlewild – Violet Vale.
They felt that they could feel
each other's thoughts.*

You know, there's no glamour in the writing life. It's like working in a mine or driving a truck. You plan your day – you put in your hours – and then you go home. If you are lucky, you don't bring it home – it's just your job and nothing more. A means by which a person can pay the bills. Pay for the paper – pay for the ink – and what remains on the table will be yours. If there's a dime in your pocket, you've had a pretty good day.

*A person under the sword of Damocles.
An author who wants to keep her character young.
A person who is falling apart at the seams.*

*"I'll dwell among
but tell no tales.
Ignore that
I am here."*

You have been – in a very practical way – an orphan?
You have been a wife?
You have been a mother?

Home – whatever that means. Exhausted and terribly sad. We pull into the driveway. Ewan is calm – no more than a carcass – as I help him out of the car.

I try not to wake up the maid as I fumble with the door.

> *All I could hear*
> *was other ones.*
> *Were thrashing in the dark.*

That her hand could reach out from the casket for one last change.

> *A kangaroo from australia - her painful doubts - what she was really like - ideal of earthly bliss - be my lifelong sorrow - a dark church spire - too beautiful to last - anything she had ever dreamed - that brief dream is over - i've imagined it thousands of times.*

> *A butcher-knife blade forged in fairyland.*
> *A robin strutting on the railing of a verandah.*
> *Daisies nodding and swaying in the pasture.*

> *Find ingleside burned down - romantic possibilities - i've never been the same since - do what was right and fair - about the real people - not the friendly haunt of daytime - give you one more chance - the secret wisdom of all mothers - yes, she was home - won't talk of this to anybody.*

This novel took a long time to plan. Doodled away the good part of a year. I just couldn't seem to find life at Ingleside. Then the children took my fancy, and things ripened up, and the writing went fast. Four months and here I am with a full first-draft. And now I will polish it as I type – it will be done in a month or two. It will serve to keep the wolf away from the door.

She had talked for eight long miles. Every other word was 'home'. But home, to her, was just a dream. Well, if her dream was to live at Green Gables, who was he to murder her dream? He'd tell his sister they didn't really need a boy.

"How horrible that artists have to be so terribly tormented."
"Some people suffer all kinds of agony and yet never manage to create a great work of art."

> *The puppet felt like a human.*
> *She wished she could walk and talk*
> *as humans do.*

> *Salvage the wreck - no matter what - episodes finding their shape - something out of balance - told him who he was - if you thought about it - clinging to a mast - to hide the scabs - only wanted dark - your life will be changed.*

And now back to the world of toil. All good things must come to an end. I must put my pen to paper once again.

Two kindred spirits
had a picnic in Hester Grey's garden.
Maude and Anne – Anne and Maude.
Birch Path – Crystal Lake.
They could hear their laughter
echo down the years.

A hurried note to Violet King. Always expecting my magnum opus. *Anne of Ingleside* won't be that, Violet. It's just a book – that's all it is – a pleasant read. It's always hard to stir up old emotions – I'd rather write about the fresh and the new. I have a few ideas for future novels. For now, I just need to rest up a bit. Perhaps my magnum opus is waiting around the bend.

So, if her brother was going to be so stubborn – turning everything upside-down and topsy-turvy on a whim – why she'd take them both in hand and introduce them both to common sense. Get both of their heads down out of the clouds and show them how to plant their feet right down firmly – all four of them – on the ground. She would have two people to manage instead of one. Serve her brother right for making such a mess of a simple plan. She'd tell her brother they didn't need a little boy.

Standing with Matthew and Marilla on the porch.
Waving to Anne as she is walking down the lane.

The puppet invented a puppet.
She made the puppet walk and talk
as humans do.

When feeling most alone - got just what he wanted - successful at what he does - clutching the wheel - see a connection - was just not there - had a pretty good day - don't lose any sleep - a backward glance - lost to the world.

I'm concerned about you, Mrs. Montgomery. You seem to want to have a talk. Is it something about your husband and your two boys?
You seem so deeply troubled, Mrs. Montgomery. Would it help if you told me more? Would it help if you were to share your darkest concerns?
Why is your journal your only confidante? Don't you know you will always have me? I am inviting you to share your burden with me.

Actually,

they were there to observe a funeral.
Anne and Maude – Maude and Anne.
Green Gables – Ingleside.
A kindred thought
had drawn them back to Avonlea.

Why do you ask so many questions? You are as inquisitive as my character, Anne. You know, Marilla wasn't too far off when she first met Anne. So many questions from such a young girl. Seemed to live with her head in the clouds. Must be nice to just follow your daydreams – like a character in a book. There's a few of us have to live down here, on the earth.

"She's had a quiet, fairly uneventful life."
"Only a writer would ever wish for anything else."

It was a world

Two friends who share each other's thoughts.
A perpetual child who dwells in Avonlea.
A girl who wonders what her future will be.

which gave the girl

You've seen the sun come up and the sun go down?
You've seen the decades come and go?
So what is your final conclusion about the nature of life?

complete control.

Tempted to write about Anne again? Well, perhaps I shall be some day. Anne is a pretty insistent little girl. Sometimes I see Anne as the exuberant driver of the buggy and myself as the tired old sorrel mare. I can enjoy her ebullient chatter – just as Matthew used to do – but at times I just want my barn and my bag of oats.

Three Books

L. M. Montgomery: I Gave You Life – a novel
In 1938, with another world war looming in the future, and with her personal problems threatening to overwhelm her, the author, L. M. Montgomery, begins to write what she has decided will be her final Anne-novel. As she works on the new novel, she recalls the days when *Anne of Green Gables* became a world-wide literary phenomenon, and the dilemma which she faced at that time: whether to write a series of Anne-novels in which Anne would remain the perpetual child which the world had come to know and to love, or to allow Anne to grow to adulthood, with all the agonizing torments of the one who had given her life – L. M. Montgomery.

The Making of *L. M. Montgomery: I Gave You Life* – a reflective journal
This journal records the author's reflections on the process of the crafting of the novel as it evolved through the stages of planning, writing, editing and polishing. It constitutes an effort to be as conscious as possible of the process whereby the single idea that suggested the topic of the novel was expanded into a complex work of art. Topics range from the nuts and bolts of novel-building to the nature of the novel as an art-form.

Planning *L. M. Montgomery: I Gave You Life* – a planning notebook
During the writing of the novel, the author kept a notebook which records the day-by-day development of the novel as it found its shape and style. The notebook reveals how a vast cluster of thoughts was sifted, selected, structured and polished into novel-form.

The Project
Together, this novel, journal and notebook comprise the twenty-fourth installment in an ongoing novel-writing project in which the author is exploring the concept of form and meaning in the novel, and of the novel as a form of expression in the 21st century. All of the published journals and notebooks are available for free at www.johnpassfield.ca.

About the Author

John Passfield was born in St. Thomas, Ontario, Canada, and continues to reside in Southern Ontario, near Cayuga, with his family. He is interested in exploring the development of the novel as an art-form, and has written many novels, planning notebooks and journals in his search for a form for the poetic novel of our time. His novel *John Passfield: Saturday Morning* was shortlisted for the ReLit Award in 2022.

Novels by John Passfield

Grave Song
The Agony of Robert Chisholm

Jumbo
P. T. Barnum's Greatest Creation

Pinafore Park
The Swan Boat Incident

Water Lane
The Pilgrimage of Christopher Marlowe

Rain of Fire
The Ordeal of Conductor Spettigue

Victoria Day
The Fabric of the Community

The Wright Brothers
Flight is Possible

Leni Riefenstahl
The Valley of the Shadow

Babe Ruth
Out of the Park

Raskolnikov
Murder with an Axe

Sergei Eisenstein
Death Day

Albert Einstein
Wonder

Geoffrey Chaucer
Canterbury Bound

Ospringe
A Visit with Grandad

Pompeii
Vesuvius Dominus

Beethoven
The Ninth Immersion

Job
The Cornerstone of the Universe

Bethune
The Only Person Alive in the World

Terry Fox
Somewhere the Hurting Must Stop

Lord and Lady Macbeth
Full of Scorpions Is My Mind

Cyril Passfield
Out West

Glenn Gould
Light and Dark

Emily Brontë
More Myself Than I

L. M. Montgomery
I Gave You Life

Pauline Johnson
Know Who I Am

John Passfield
Saturday Morning

Eleonora Duse
Let Me Have My Wings

James McIntyre
The Mammoth Cheese

Shakespeare and Cleopatra
My Life Is Not My Own

John and Santa
The Cowboy Shirt

John and Cassandra
Fair is Fair

John and Dickens
A Christmas Mystery

John and Lewis Carroll
Wonder Fall

John and Mother Goose
The Carnival of Tales

John and the Universan
Nothing is Known

See www.johnpassfield.ca for publishing information.

In Search of Form and Meaning: Journals by John Passfield

Each journal is a day-by-day record of the complex process that a writer undergoes while crafting a work of art. It records the largest decisions, of structure and theme, and the smallest decisions, such as the choice of one word over another, and the constant interaction between the two. Each journal is a record of a writer's reflection on the craft of novel-writing.

The Making of Grave Song

The Making of Jumbo

The Making of Pinafore Park

The Making of Water Lane

The Making of Rain of Fire

The Making of Victoria Day

The Making of Flight is Possible

The Making of The Valley of the Shadow

The Making of Out of the Park

The Making of Murder with an Axe

The Making of Death Day

The Making of Wonder

The Making of Canterbury Bound

The Making of Ospringe

The Making of Vesuvius Dominus

The Making of The Ninth Immersion

The Making of The Cornerstone of the Universe

The Making of The Only Person Alive in the World

The Making of Somewhere the Hurting Must Stop

The Making of Full of Scorpions Is My Mind

The Making of Out West

The Making of Glenn Gould: Light and Dark

The Making of Emily Brontë: More Myself Than I

The Making of Pauline Johnson: Know Who I Am

The Making of John Passfield: Saturday Morning

The Making of Eleonora Duse: Let Me Have My Wings

The Making of James McIntyre: The Mammoth Cheese

The Making of Shakespeare and Cleopatra: My Life Is Not My Own

The Making of John and Santa: The Cowboy Shirt

The Making of John and Cassandra: Fair is Fair

The Making of John and Dickens: A Christmas Mystery

The Making of John and Lewis Carroll: Wonder Fall

The Making of John and Mother Goose: The Carnival of Tales

The Making of John and the Universan: Nothing is Known

See www.johnpassfield.ca for publishing information.

The Novel as an Art-Form: Planning Notebooks by John Passfield

Each planning notebook is a printed version of the hand-written notebook which records the planning, writing, editing and polishing of each novel. Each notebook is an attempt to record, understand, and organize the vast cluster of thoughts which occur as one grapples with the various levels of organization which a clear yet complex work of art demands.

Planning Grave Song

Planning Jumbo

Planning Pinafore Park

Planning Water Lane

Planning Rain of Fire

Planning Victoria Day

Planning Flight is Possible

Planning The Valley of the Shadow

Planning Out of the Park

Planning Murder with an Axe

Planning Death Day

Planning Wonder

Planning Canterbury Bound

Planning Ospringe

Planning Vesuvius Dominus

Planning The Ninth Immersion

Planning The Cornerstone of the Universe

Planning The Only Person Alive in the World

Planning Somewhere the Hurting Must Stop

Planning Full of Scorpions Is My Mind

Planning Out West

Planning Glenn Gould: Light and Dark

Planning Emily Brontë: More Myself Than I

Planning L. M. Montgomery: I Gave You Life

Planning Pauline Johnson: Know Who I Am

Planning John Passfield: Saturday Morning

Planning Eleonora Duse: Let Me Have My Wings

Planning James McIntyre: The Mammoth Cheese

Planning Shakespeare and Cleopatra: My Life Is Not My Own

Planning John and Santa: The Cowboy Shirt

Planning John and Cassandra: Fair is Fair

Planning John and Dickens: A Christmas Mystery

Planning John and Lewis Carroll: Wonder Fall

Planning John and Mother Goose: The Carnival of Tales

Planning John and the Universan: Nothing is Known

See www.johnpassfield.ca for publishing information.

Other Books by John Passfield

Oak Street
The Passfield Family

The Poetic Novel I
Influences and Elements

Intensities I
Verses on Various Topics

Intensities II
Verses on Various Topics

Deepening Imagery I
Verses from the Novels

Deepening Imagery II
Verses from the Novels

Deepening Imagery III
Verses from the Novels

Deepening Imagery IV
Verses from the Novels

Video-notes I
(1–100)

Video-notes II
(101–200)

See www.johnpassfield.ca for free access.

www.ingramcontent.com/pod-product-compliance
Lightning Source LLC
Chambersburg PA
CBHW031119080526
44587CB00011B/1038